THE
GLASSES
WE

WEAR

Reflections

On Christian

Worldview

Contents

To my Dad,
Whose faithful service and teaching helped give me the
glasses I wear

INTRODUCTION

*"What comes into our minds when we think about God is
the most important thing about us."*
– A. W. Tozer, The Knowledge of the Holy

THE *GLASSES WE Wear* is an exploration of Christian
apologetics, worldview, and perspective. Although not
one of the ideas in this book is new, I hope that I have presented them in a way that causes a shift in thinking from short
term to long term, from the temporal to the eternal, away from
self and toward God. We will consider the Christian perspective
on many topics, including salvation, happiness, purpose, creation, death, and trials.

Numerous excellent books deal exhaustively with the evidence for the Christian faith, and I have been blessed by many of
them. But I am neither a scholar nor an academic. My purpose
here is not to provide a comprehensive investigation that lays out
"proofs" for the Christian faith but rather to encourage a reflective

engagement with the Christian worldview. So, essentially, this is a "worldview devotional." Meditating on God and His Word is fast becoming a lost art in this busy culture of ours. I want to take some time to dwell on God, think about who He is, and discover who we are in relationship to Him.

My aim is to provoke you to think about God and then, in response to your realization of God, experience a shift in your perspective on life and, ultimately, find in Jesus Christ salvation and restoration for your soul.

Any discussion about God must begin with humility, in realizing that we don't have all the answers, that we don't need all the answers, and that we cannot comprehend all the answers. We approach this topic not perched high on the seat of judgment but rather bowed low in reverence. If there is no God, life amounts to a cruel cosmic prank that places within us a deep desire for meaning and purpose and yet gives us absolutely none. If this is the case then nature mocks us, laughing at our feeble attempts to find direction in the pitch blackness of futility. On the other hand, if there is a God . . . *Oh my God!* . . . how great and vast and marvelous You must be! This changes everything! How does the reality of God change my life? What if this God is interested in us – in *me* – and actually cares for us – for *me*? Who is this God? And who are we as people that He is mindful of us?

I invite you to join with me in reflecting on this amazing God, enjoying the wonder of His revelation, and pondering in awe His incomprehensibility.

IMPLICATIONS OF WORLDVIEW

"...having the eyes of your hearts enlightened, that you
may know what is the hope to which he has called you...."
(Ephesians 1:18 ESV)

W E ALL WEAR glasses. No, I'm not talking about eyeglasses with lenses and frames that loop over the bridge of our nose and the crest of our ears. The glasses I am referring to fit not on the head but on the heart. Just as eyeglasses improve our visual acuity, so the glasses of the heart allow us to see life itself more clearly. That is, as long as the prescription is correct. Just as different people wear different eyeglasses made from different prescriptions, so different people wear different *heart* glasses. The world can appear drastically different from one person to the next depending on which glasses we are wearing. Everyone has a worldview, a pair of glasses through which they view and interpret life. If we are consistent, we will apply the same worldview in every facet of life.

But, that is where I see a real problem. Take, for example, an atheistic/naturalistic worldview, in which there is no God or anything else supernatural. This is the pair of glasses many people claim they wear when interpreting science and the rest of life as a whole. But is it *really*? Does the atheist really wear these glasses *all* the time? If he is consistent, then he should, right? Most would probably answer with a resounding "Yes!" But let's take a closer look at just what that would mean.

Let's consider an example from the hallways of a typical high school (or college). When the bell rings a group of students leave their biology class where they just learned how primordial sludge produced the first living cells. Last semester they learned how the universe came into being from nothing and will one day return to nothing. They walk down the hall to history class where they listen to the teacher lecture about the atrocities of the Holocaust and all the horrific things the Nazis did during that time, murdering 6,000,000 or more Jews.

Now let's pretend that a student keeps a consistent worldview during both biology and history classes. The student raises her hand and says, "Atrocity? The Holocaust is no more an atrocity than the blue whale eating millions of krill every day!" Now this is an incredibly insensitive, uneducated, and racist comment – that just happens to be entirely consistent with an atheistic worldview. The atheist/naturalist has no ground whatsoever to value human life above any other life. Humans do not enjoy any special status or position in a naturalistic world. After all, evolutionarily speaking, the krill is just as modern a creature as a human being, each following their own unique path over billions of year to reach their current form.

In the Christian worldview what makes us humans valuable is the fact that we are created in the image of God. The Bible says that God Himself breathed life into Adam, which is in stark contrast to the story of human origins we find in secular science. I find absolutely nothing special or unique about human life in the atheistic worldview, except perhaps that we were extremely good at overcoming astronomical odds to exist in the first place.

I would not consider humans or any other living thing on earth "lucky," though, because living in this world of suffering for a short time and then descending back into an eternal nothingness is one of the most depressing scenarios I can imagine. It is certainly not born out of luck – irony perhaps, but not luck. (It is ironic that, given the atheists' profoundly bleak outlook on life, a movement was started some years ago to refer to atheists as "Brights").

Back to the "atrocity" of the Holocaust. There can be no such thing as evil or good in a meaningless universe. There is no right. There is no wrong. There is no ought. There just *is*. There is no standard to measure one set of morals against another. The atheist has no more moral authority to judge the Nazis for gassing Jews than he does to judge the blue whale for eating krill.

This is what atheists – *if they are consistent* – will see as they observe the world. It is utterly depressing and morally bankrupt. I do not believe, however, that most atheists are amoral. Most probably hold human life to be of greater value than animal life and believe in right and wrong, at least on a basic level. They are just terribly inconsistent. The atheist can indeed live by a set of morals, and most do; those morals, however, cannot be judged as better or superior to any other morals because there is no ultimate standard against which to judge them.

The glasses we wear in science class affect *everything* else in our lives. We cannot live in just one compartment of life at a time. What we believe about science affects what we believe about politics, economics, relationships, marriage, recreation, and everything else. It affects how we view the value of life and the purpose and meaning behind it. Jesus said, "You cannot serve two masters." You cannot serve one master in the science classroom and then turn and serve another in the history classroom.

The Christian wears an entirely different set of glasses. When your worldview starts with God (all worldviews start either with the absence of God or with the presence of God) you have a foundation to build upon. There are absolutes. There is right and wrong. There is good and evil. Our hearts are screaming this truth to us daily as our conscience bears witness to our own behavior and to the evil and suffering in the world around us. What we think about God always comes first (whether we are atheistic or theistic). It is foundational to everything else. Though we acknowledge that there are many different atheist worldviews and many different theist worldviews, all worldviews must begin with the fundamental choice: God or no God. The worldview we choose must remain consistent. If there is no God in science, there can be no God in history or in politics or in law and morals. What we see depends on the glasses we wear. Which glasses will you choose?

The Glasses We Wear

We all have impairments that damage our sight,
Our vision is cloudy, weak, and dim.

This blindness is deeper than reflecting light,
It covers our hearts deep within.

Choosing our glasses, we hope to see better,
Viewing the world, looking for sense.
The story of life down to the last letter,
Interpreted through our selected lens.

Do we see clearly, the view from God's eyes,
Or rely on a man-made correction?
Are we accepting of truth or lies,
Who is to point in the right direction?

God's clear view is given from above,
By His Spirit the willing heart will open.
Before the world chosen in love,
His Son, Jesus to put our hope in.

Seeing this world from eternity's view,
We find meaning along life's way
God's vision gives perspective anew,
A promise for a better day.

Reflection

❶ What is your worldview? Have you ever taken time to consider which set of glasses you are wearing?

❷ Are you ever tempted to change glasses depending on the situation? If so, when and why?

❸ Where does your worldview come from?

- 2 -

OUT OF TIME

"I am the Alpha and the Omega,
the first and the last,
the beginning and the end."
(Revelation 22:13 ESV)

TWO-THOUSAND YEARS IS a long time to wait. Some would say the events that took place during the life of Jesus are now ancient history and have no meaning for us today. How could the teaching of one simple peasant from a small village in ancient Israel be relevant for us? Does the life that He lived or the death that He died really mean anything for modern people? That was so long ago, so much has changed, so much has been discovered, Jesus has still not returned, and life just carries on as it always has. Couldn't it be said that time, all by itself, without the need for any other evidence, has debunked the claims of Christianity? This is the argument predicted in 2 Peter 3:4 (ESV):

"They will say, 'Where is the promise of his coming? For ever since the fathers fell asleep, all things are continuing as they were from the beginning of creation.'"

According to God, it was not long ago when Jesus came to this earth. I'm not suggesting that God has rewritten history. From a human perspective, the earth has indeed run its course many times around the sun since Jesus walked among us. The point is that God does not measure time the way we do. God is not bound by time. As humans we experience the present, remember the past, and look toward the future. We are quite literally prisoners of the moment. We cannot change our past and we do not know the future. With God, it is not this way. God created time for the benefit of His creation. He does not need it!

God existed before time began. He is not ruled by time the way you and I are. He is no more bound by the passing of time than He is held by the pull of gravity. The entirety of history from beginning to end is in His view. God is not caught up in the swift current of time, being pulled downstream farther and farther from past events, never knowing what lies ahead. No, instead He stands on the shore of the river seeing both the headwaters springing forth and the final culmination as the river completes its course, emptying into the ocean of eternity.

The clock is not ticking on God. Time is not running out for Him to make His move. He does not feel the pressure of 2,000 years. History is unfolding before Him just the way He saw it from before the earth experienced its first sunrise.

Each moment is present to God. The past is not far behind and the future is not far ahead. If God is really outside of time, it means that the incarnation, death, and resurrection of Jesus are very present events to Him, as are creation and the last battle.

This means that when we complain, "Where is God?" or "Why does God take so long?" we are asking very human questions that arise from our captivity to the limits of time. God can rightly say that the cross is a current event. He can also rightly say that He is *not* slow to fulfill His promises. Peter is quick to respond to the critics present in his own day:

> *"But do not overlook this one fact, beloved, that with the Lord one day is as a thousand years, and a thousand years as one day. The Lord is not slow to fulfill his promise as some count slowness, but is patient toward you, not wishing that any should perish, but that all should reach repentance." (2 Peter 3:8-9 ESV)*

"One day is as a thousand years, and a thousand years as one day." What an eloquent description of God's relationship to time. And how difficult it is, in the frailty of our human minds, for us to grasp this profound truth! At the same time, how freeing it is to realize that God is The Almighty and that none of the forces that we are subject to reign over Him at all! If God is this great, and this powerful, and if He cares for you and me, that fact should bring a profound peace to our hearts.

God is not slow. He has not forgotten. God *is* out of time because He transcends time, but He is not *out of time* to fulfill His promises.

Time

Did you begin,
 Or have you always been?
  To where are you going?
   The future view is dim.

What great mystery,
  Through all the ages,
    Befuddles philosophy,
      And baffles the sages.

Created by God,
  Or always the same?
    Who has made you,
      Infinite span or finite days?

Making foolish the wise,
  Where is the knowledge of men?
    Blinding our eyes,
      To when you did begin.

Eternally present?
  Or commanded, "Commence!"
    Something from nothing
      Or something from Him?

What is eternal,
  Spirit or matter?
    Is life merely temporal,
      Or are we made for hereafter?

God outside of time,
  Each moment present to Him,
    Acknowledge creator or creation,
      Reveals our hearts within.

Reflection

❶ How does pondering time help you to see God differently?

❷ If God is outside of time, how does He show patience towards us?

❸ Could it be that time's clock has always been running? Or do you think time began at a certain point?

- 3 -

WHERE IS GOD?

"WHY DOESN'T GOD do something?" Skeptics and believers alike ask this common question. From our perspective, it seems that a "good God" would be more involved, intervening often to make the world a better place and prevent human suffering. The idea behind this poem is that in large part what God *is* doing was done on the cross. God's salvation plan consists of more than just making life better for us today. It is actually the re-making of our lifeless souls and a restoration of His perfect creation. It is a complete salvation, not just partial or temporary, and it had to begin with the cross.

Where is God through all our pain,
Through sadness and darkness, and while evil reigns?
Where is God when tears and grief,
Steal our joy and rob us of peace?

God of power,
　　Why hide Your face?
　　　　When the world is collapsing,
　　　　　　Have we misplaced our faith?

If You care,
　　Why leave us alone?
　　　　These burdens to bear,
　　　　　　Is Your heart callous stone?

Do You see the suffering?
　　Do You feel the hunger?
　　　　Does Your justice not burn,
　　　　　　Against the wicked man's plunder?

Look within,
　　Our hearts run from You.
　　　　This world of sin,
　　　　　　Our wages due.

O, Timeless One,
　　O, Ancient of Days,
　　　　Your heart is not cold,
　　　　　　Nor do You turn Your gaze.

But stepping,
　　Into time as man,
　　　　You made a way,
　　　　　　You had a plan.

To rescue hearts,
　　Turned from You,
　　　　Hung on the cross,
　　　　　　The penalty due.

So where is God,
  Does He not care?
    He is on the cross.
      Our burdens to bear.

Once for all,
  To wipe out sin,
    To rid the earth,
      Of evil without and within.

Rising in victory,
  New life to bring,
    O, death, now,
      Where is your sting?

We are not left,
  In this life alone.
    But invited,
      To ever gather around the throne.

O, God You know our hearts
  Give us faith,
    To see You as You are,
      And to marvel at Your grace.

Reflection

❶ Does it seem that God is not active in our world today?

❷ If God is real, how do you think His perspective would be different from ours?

❸ How does the sacrifice of Jesus change your worldview? Does the fact that God Himself in Jesus experienced suffering change your answer to the question "Why doesn't God do something?"

- 4 -

BELIEVING IS SEEING

*"What matters most is not the state of the evidence,
but the state of the heart."*

CHRISTIAN APOLOGETICS SHOWS us that belief in God is a legitimate intellectual position based upon philosophical reasoning, scientific evidence, and historical documentation. The Apostle Paul tells us in Romans chapter one that the attributes of God have been on display through the creation of the world since the beginning of time. Therefore, we have no excuse for denying God. This of course begs the questions: "Why doesn't everyone believe? And if God is so evident, then what role does faith play? Do we believe because we have proof, or do we believe because we have faith?"

When we look to God's Word (the Bible) we can start to find answers to these questions. God values our faith. Consider a few examples. In the Gospel of Matthew, a centurion (a Roman military commander) asked Jesus to heal his servant even though Jesus was some distance from the home where the servant lay sick. Jesus commended him for his faith saying, "Truly I tell you, with no one in Israel have I found such faith" (Matthew 8:5-13). When presenting Himself to Thomas after the resurrection, Jesus said, "Have you believed because you have seen me? Blessed are those who have not seen and yet have believed" (John 20:29). And when the children gathered around Him, Jesus said, "Let the little children come to me . . . for to such belongs the kingdom of God" (Mark 10:13-15), an apparent reference to child-like faith. In Romans (Paul's letter to the Christians in Rome), Paul stated that it was Abraham's faith that made him righteous before God. The writer of the book of Hebrews takes us through the famous "Heroes of Faith" passage in chapter eleven. There are many other examples of faith on display in the New and Old Testaments. It is clear that God puts a high value on people having faith in Him.

Why does God want us to show faith? Because faith reveals the state of our hearts. When interacting with people, Jesus always cut to the "heart" of the issue. He always sought the inner motives of those He came in contact with. Take the example of the rich young ruler who came to Jesus to ask what he must do to inherit eternal life. He boldly declared that he had kept the entire law and yet he still sensed that he lacked something. Jesus quickly teased out the real issue, which was the young man's greed, and he left sorrowful because he could not part with his material wealth (Matthew 19:16-22). Jesus put more emphasis on the heart and what lies within it than on outward appearance (which was His central criticism of the Pharisees, the religious leaders of the day). Understanding this is important if we are going to answer the question "Why do we believe?"

"For the LORD sees not as man sees: man looks on the outward appearance, but the LORD looks on the heart."
(1 Samuel 16:7 ESV)

God is interested in our hearts. He wants our hearts to be in a certain condition. In Scripture, the humble heart is commended while the proud heart is condemned. Do you have a humble child-like heart that believes without question or a proud, hardened heart that seeks proof?

"What God declares the believing heart confesses without the need of further proof. Indeed to seek proof is to admit doubt and to obtain proof is to render faith superfluous."
–A.W. Tozer

A humble heart requires faith, and faith requires trust. Where do we place our trust? In the power of our intellect? Or do we perhaps trust the power of the evidence? Or is it in God and His Word? Trusting God is simply a matter of seeing Him for who He is: the sovereign Creator and sustainer of the universe. In Colossians 1:15-17 Paul wrote this concerning Jesus:

"He is the image of the invisible God, the firstborn of all creation. For by him all things were created, in heaven and on earth, visible and invisible, whether thrones or dominions or rulers or authorities – all things were created through him and for him. And he is before all things, and in him all things hold together."

This one verse should be enough. If that is our God, how can we not trust Him?

Think of this in terms of our daily lives. We place our faith in individuals all the time just because of who they are. Every time

I fly in an airplane, I put faith in the person operating the aircraft. Do I understand everything about aeronautics? No, but I trust that the pilot does because of who he or she is. We put faith in doctors, contractors, and professionals of every sort, not because we understand all they are doing but because of their title, position, and identity in their respective field. It is the same way with God. Once we come to realize that God is God we trust Him, not because we understand everything He does, but because we know who He is. Do we understand all the ways of God? No, but since He spoke the universe into existence perhaps we should give Him the benefit of the doubt.

If faith is so central to our belief, what role does the evidence play? Is there any *reason* to believe? What role does apologetics play? Certainly the evidence is there. The letter to the Romans tells us it is there for all to see. Why doesn't the evidence compel everyone to bend their knee in reverence to God? The answer, once again, lies in the state of the heart. Turning back to Romans, we learn that men by their "unrighteousness, suppress the truth" (Romans 1:18). The truth is evident, but some refuse to accept it. Their "foolish hearts are darkened" and "claiming to be wise" they "became fools" (Romans 1:21-22). When we do not "see fit to acknowledge God" (Romans 1:28), that is the work of arrogant human pride.

> *"For you save a humble people, but the haughty eyes you bring down." (Psalm 18:27 ESV)*

C. S. Lewis, in *Mere Christianity*, describes pride in this way:

> *"In God you come up against something which is in every respect immeasurably superior to yourself. Unless you know God as that – and, therefore, know yourself as*

nothing in comparison – you do not know God at all. As long as you are proud you cannot know God. A proud man is always looking down on things and people: and, of course, as long as you are looking down, you cannot see something that is above you."

Christian apologetics will not stir a proud heart to repentance no matter how strong and convincing the evidence may be. What matters most is not the state of the evidence, but the state of the heart. The intellectual seeks to understand. Of course, understanding in itself is not wrong, but seeking to elevate human reasoning to the level of the infinite God is absurd. Skeptics will withhold their trust in God because they do not agree with nor understand the ways of the Almighty. In other words, "claiming to be wise, they became fools."

Even the most compelling evidence may fail to convince a hardened heart. Remember the story Jesus told about the rich man and Lazarus. After he had died and found himself in Hades, the rich man was having a conversation with Abraham. He begged Abraham to send Lazarus to his brothers so they could be warned and repent. What did Abraham tell him? "If they do not hear Moses and the Prophets, neither will they be convinced if someone should rise from the dead" (Luke 16:19-31 ESV). In the same way, the Jewish leaders witnessed first-hand many miracles that Jesus performed, and yet their hearts were hardened, and instead of believing they began to devise a plot to kill him. Friedrich Nietzsche, who is credited with the phrase "God is dead," was a champion of atheism who lived in the 19th century. He is quoted as saying, "It is our preference that decides against Christianity, not arguments." He was repelled by the very idea of

God and thus rejected any evidence that supported Christian belief.

So what do we do with all this compelling evidence found in the discipline of Christian apologetics? We cannot argue a soul into the Kingdom of Heaven. God opens hearts, not arguments. Without God's first loving us, we would not seek Him, see Him, or know Him. I think the evidence is primarily useful for reinforcing the faith of believers, helping them to better understand who God is, and allowing them to have a coherent answer when critics question their belief. In some cases, it may indeed remove a roadblock for a seeker and enable that person to take the first step of faith. But for the most part apologetics is for Christians.

A scene from the movie *Indiana Jones and the Last Crusade* will help us to understand how God opens the eyes of those who believe. In a scene at the end of the movie Indy was trying to rescue his father by passing through three challenges to find the Holy Grail. The final challenge was to step out in faith over a large cavernous expanse. Indy could not see any bridge, rope, or other help to cross to the other side. It seemed certain he would plummet to his death if he tried to jump. But he took a step of faith, and what did he find? A rock solid bridge that led to the other side. His faith was rewarded as his eyes were opened to see that which was hidden before. Only when we accept the greatness of God by faith, with a humble heart, can we begin to understand the evidence that so clearly reveals His presence.

It takes a softened heart to respond in faith to the Holy Spirit's call to repentance. The Scripture both shows and tells us that faith is of primary importance while evidence is secondary. When we do accept God and the work of Jesus by faith, however, we can find a solid foundation of truth based not in fairy tales but in reality undergirded with compelling evidence. This solid foundation is not just spiritual but physical in terms of the evidence found in history, science, and philosophy.

On a personal note, apologetics have changed my life and the way I view my faith. I have come to see God more clearly and more reverently than ever before. Child-like faith is commendable, and many Christians are content to believe without investigating the "reasons" to believe. In some ways, though, this is missing out on part of the gift we have been given. It is like receiving a gift on Christmas from someone special and accepting it with joy and thankfulness, but then never opening it and exploring the contents in detail. The gift God has given to us in Jesus Christ is simply incredible. Receive it with joy, but do not hesitate to explore the inner workings of Christianity by learning about the bedrock foundation God has laid in convincing evidence. Just like Indy, take that first step and then see the solid rock on which you stand.

". . . but in your hearts honor Christ the Lord as holy, always being prepared to make a defense to anyone who asks you for a reason for the hope that is in you; yet do it with gentleness and respect. . . ." (1 Peter 3:15 ESV)

Reflection

❶ Does your belief come mostly from faith or mostly from the evidence?

❷ Is it wrong to seek proof of Christianity?

❸ How and why did the early Church respond to the Gospel? Did they have proof?

❹ Discuss pride versus humility in approaching the subject of God.

5

IF *I* WAS GOD

"If there is no God, then there are no answers.
If there is a God, then He doesn't answer to you."

THIS WORLD IS a hard place to live. There is sickness, hunger, abuse, wars, disasters, horrific crimes, and injustice of every sort. Many look at the world today and conclude that there is no God. After all, if there was a God, surely He would do *something*. Right?

Suffering and injustice are not evidence against the existence of God. The fact that this world is a hard place to live does not strengthen the atheist's case. Suffering and injustice do bring into question the character of God, which is an entirely different topic that assumes God's existence. In other words, you cannot question God's existence by criticizing His behavior. It would be like saying, "I don't believe the Rolling Stones were ever a real band because I don't like any of their music" or "I don't like impressionist paintings, so Van Gogh never existed." Nonsense.

Critics often look at our world today and presume upon God's character because He is not conducting Himself in the way that we as humans would. This amounts to humanizing God and trying to judge Him according to our standards as finite beings. It is an "If I were God, then. . ." argument, which is attractive as low-hanging fruit to throw at believers but ultimately fails under scrutiny. The reason it fails is because we human beings are not God. If there was a God, He would be so vastly different from us in every conceivable way as to be incomprehensible. Our criticism of God is similar to a mouse's criticizing the mathematics of an astrophysicist—only the gap between us humans and God is infinitely wider than the gap between a mouse and the astrophysicist!

So the question "Why doesn't God do things my way?" is dead on arrival. In Scripture God tells us, "my thoughts are not your thoughts, neither are your ways my ways" (Isaiah 55:8). The God who has revealed Himself to us through the Bible said this, but wouldn't it be true even if God had never said it? God, by definition, is not on our playing field, and yet this fact is often forgotten.

Now let's turn back to the question of suffering and injustice. These are very real issues that we simply cannot ignore. If a person cannot disprove God, perhaps he can at least discredit Him. Perhaps he can show Him to be inept, uncaring, or aloof. Or maybe He is a cruel being who enjoys seeing pain in the creation? Maybe He wants to fix things but simply lacks the ability to do so?

If not for God's revelation, all of these possibilities would be open to debate and discussion. If God had never communicated with us, we would be left to ponder these questions. The Christian worldview, which is based in and on God's revelation, is the best explanation for the circumstances we see in the world today. Christians are best able to explain suffering. In contrast, an atheistic worldview falls short of explaining our drive to make moral distinctions, to designate some behaviors just and others as less just, some behaviors as right and others less right.

The concept of suffering implies that things are "not the way they should be," which is a statement the atheist can never make and stay consistent to his or her foundational beliefs. There is no "ought" for the atheist. In other words, an atheist cannot claim that things "ought" to be a certain way. In fact, they cannot assign value or purpose to anything because everything is meaningless and without ultimate purpose. In a strange sort of way, the recognition of suffering and injustice actually point as evidence for God, not against God. We need a standard of straight to know what crooked looks like.

God's revelation tells us that there is suffering in the world because of sin. Things are not right. There is in fact an "ought," and we are not in it. This is *not* what God intended. There is a Creator God who is all powerful, loving, just, engaged, and relational. He created us for relationship and we chose to forsake that relationship and set out to make our way alone. Our decision separated us from Him forever, and caused this world of pain in which we all currently live. But despite our going astray, God had a plan for redemption and restoration.

We were created in the "image of God" with "eternity set in our hearts." Yet everyone knows something is wrong in the world and something is also wrong inside each of us. We are in search of fulfillment that is elusive to describe and even more elusive to find. We search for it in money, status, accomplishment, drugs, sex, family, relationships, work, service, "do-gooding," and a host of other false pursuits. What we are missing is that relationship with our Creator for which we were created. God sent His Son, Jesus, into this world as a man with a two-fold purpose: to reveal and to restore. Jesus Christ is the one who reveals God to us. It is in Jesus that we can find out what God is like. He is also the one through whom we are restored to a relationship with God that fulfills our ultimate desires.

As anyone can see, the restoration is incomplete. God, however, is "doing something." Jesus has come, believing hearts have been made new, but still we wait for the restoration of creation including our physical bodies. We still wait for the end of suffering and injustice. Just as God's Word promised a coming Savior to rescue our souls, so it promises a returning Savior to set all things right that are wrong in this world. Come, Lord Jesus, come!

Reflection

❶ Do you ever wonder what you would do if you were God?

❷ Why do you think God does things so differently than we would?

❸ Why do we try to humanize God?

6

THINGS HE HAS MADE

S CIENTISTS HAVE DETERMINED that there are hundreds of constants in our universe that must be set with pinpoint precision, both individually and in relationship to one another, in order for our universe to exist and to allow an earth that supports life. The speed of light, the gravitational force, the size of the moon, the size of the sun, the distance from the earth to the sun, and even the tilt of the earth are just a few examples of constants that must be set exactly as they are. This is the "fine tuning" of the universe, and it is undeniable. We have either won the cosmic lottery 1,000,000 times over, or there is a God who designed this place with human beings in mind. This poem is a reflection of God's great design.

God, the great architect over creation,
  Spoke in the universe grand design.

Such precision and balance deserves meditation,
Filling with wonder this heart of mine.

In the beginning, with wisdom He spoke,
Commanding the darkness retreat from the light.
Fixed the sun in the sky and the first morning broke.
The stars, each one lit, to shine in the night.

The moon so faithfully, in orbit tracks,
Marking the months and changing the tides.
Neither beauty nor function this handiwork lacks,
Bringing glory and light when full in the skies.

Gravity's strength is holding us all,
The Maker's fine tuning spot on.
No change is harmless, even though small,
The slightest difference and all life is gone.

Twenty-three the earth's tilt in degrees,
Suspended in space by the Word of His power.
Who can fathom the blueprint God sees?
Planned each rotation, counting each hour.

God covers us in atmosphere,
As if His hands encircle the earth.
Letting only what is needed clear,
His perfect protection shows our worth.

Between earth and sun He set a span,
If greater too cold, and if less too hot.
Another part of His master plan,
Anything different and life would be naught.

Thousands of details set with care,
Obvious for all who will look.

Those with eyes open will see him there,
Revealed in not just The Book

This world where we live is a special place,
The foundations He crafted in brilliance are laid.
Not just a home but revealing His face,
Speaking the truth by the things He has made.

Reflection

❶ Do both the Christian and the atheist have faith?

❷ Is there a difference between the faith of an atheist and the faith of a Christian? If so, describe the difference?

❸ Our existence is extraordinary. How does this change your life?

– 7 –

THINKING ABOUT NOTHING

L ET'S THINK ABOUT nothing for a few minutes . . . . No, really. Let's think about what nothing is or isn't and how it impacts our lives today. Nothing is that which does not exist. It is something that isn't. Nothing is anything that isn't something. Are we confused yet? Nothing has no form or feature. In it, there is no space or time. There is no color or dimension; no lookout from which it can be viewed. There are no laws that rule it and no ideas that form it. No plan directs it, and no direction guides it. It simply isn't there. Aristotle said that, "Nothing is what rocks dream about." It is hard to comprehend, really. For a finite human mind, pondering nothing is like pondering eternity. There are some concepts that just don't compute well in our minds and *nothing* is one of them.

And yet, from this utter emptiness, I am asked to believe that time, space, matter, natural law, moral law, planets, stars, solar systems, our sun, our earth, simple life, complex life, emotion, consciousness, meaning, and everything else you can think or imagine came into being out of shear happenstance from . . . nothing. It would take some serious faith to believe that.

The naturalist may claim that the above premise is false because he or she believes that nature's laws, matter, space, and time are eternal or have been present always in some form. Maybe there was no "nothingness" prior to the beginning of the universe as we know it. But, isn't this just elevating the natural realm to the level of the infinite God? We all worship something – either Creator or creation. Either the creation is infinite or the Creator is infinite. For the naturalist, there is a god; it is just called by a different name – Mother Nature – if you will. In this case, atheism (which means *disbelief in the existence of a supreme being or beings*) is a misnomer. The convenient feature of the god of nature is that she does not require any moral responsibility and lays no claim to the rule of creation or its inhabitants. There is no personality or love. No principles, really. That gives us the freedom to decide right and wrong for ourselves. In fact, everyone is right, so long as he or she is *sincere*.

But let's return to nothing for a moment. Can something come from nothing? Common sense says, "No!" I believe that something (everything, really) came not from some*thing* but from some*body*. Out of God's infinite love He created. He created the universe and human beings to share in that eternal love. When we rebelled against God and sat ourselves as usurpers on the throne of authority over our own lives, God did not turn away. Rather, He intervened, sending His own Son into space and time as a human being to suffer and die and pay the penalty that we rebels all deserve. He did this so the relationship between

Himself and His creation could be restored. In this personal, infinite, and loving God, I believe . . . and nothing less.

Reflection

❶ What is eternal? What has always been and what will always be?

❷ Do you find "nothing" a difficult concept to grasp?

❸ Why is the idea of nothingness problematic for skeptics?

8

PERCEPTION IS REALITY ... EXCEPT WHEN IT IS NOT

ERCEPTION IS REALITY. In order to understand the sum of this saying, we must first examine the parts. Perception carries multiple definitions, but an accurate summary could be *an awareness of or appreciation for the surrounding environment.*

Reality is something that exists. It is something that is really there. Reality does not depend on one's interpretation, nor is it subject to one's preference, it just simply *is.*

The origin of this phrase is traced to a campaign advisor to George H. W. Bush. In politics, the presentation of the candidate is all important, the reality behind the candidate is less so. How the public perceives the candidate will become the basis on which they cast their votes. Their perception of the candidate becomes their "reality." The trick for the campaign advisors is to manipulate the perception until the desired reality is reached and a favorable vote is cast. In this situation a better term would be "deception" because changing people's perception through manipulation causes them to believe in something that is *not* real. It is lying. Fortunately the focus of this chapter is not politics!

"Perception is reality" as used in conversation today means that our behavior is influenced by what we determine to be true at any given time. Consider the example of a paranoid person whose perception is that "Everyone is out to get me!" This perception causes a set of behaviors that are consistent with that belief.

Our perception is all important because it will determine the actions we take in the real world. As in the example of the paranoid person, it does not matter if the perception is accurate or not; the fact is what we perceive to be true will direct our behavior and decisions in everyday life. A man standing in his driveway may duck for cover when he hears the backfire of a passing car. Another man serving in a military combat zone may also duck for cover when he hears a loud noise. Both of these men had a similar experience and responded similarly in ducking for cover. One, however, was perfectly safe and the other had reason to fear for his life. The point is this: Perceptions can change, but reality does not. The reality (safety in one case and danger in the other) existed independent of either man's experience. Perception can be manipulated; reality cannot.

Consider this idea applied to the spiritual realm. What is the general perception when it comes to spiritual matters? The most obvious answer is that the spiritual world is subjective at best and unreal at worst. The perception is that God is far off and spiritual truth is evasive. This perception leads to a focus on our temporal lives and the material world. Instead of looking forward to eternity, we look at today and try to gain as much comfort and pleasure as possible. Our hope is placed in this life instead of in the life to come.

In God's Word we learn that there is a spiritual reality. People tend to ignore, deny, or distort this truth with consequences that carry into eternity. Spiritual reality is close at hand. It is not some far off, mystical fantasy. Just as the Vice President is one heart-beat away from the presidency, so we are one heartbeat away from the full realization of our spiritual reality. It is literally one breath away. One of God's attributes is omnipresence. He is present everywhere as David beautifully described in Psalm 139. Even though invisible, He is nevertheless active and real. He is there, working behind the scenes, to accomplish His purposes in this world. The enemy, Satan, is also at work. He is not omnipres-ent and lacks God's omnipotence, but he is indeed a force to be reckoned with. There is an ever-present spiritual battle raging on between the forces of good and the forces of evil. If we were to see it, even just briefly, it would change our lives forever.

Let's consider some examples from Scripture. In 2 Kings, the Syrian king had surrounded the city of Dothan with the intent of capturing and killing the prophet Elisha:

> *"When the servant of the man of God rose early in the morning and went out, behold, an army with horses and chariots was all around the city. And the servant said, 'Alas, my master! What shall we do?' He said, 'Do not be afraid, for those who are with us are more than those who are with them.' Then Elisha prayed and said, 'O Lord, please open his eyes that he may see.' So the Lord opened the eyes of the young man, and he saw, and behold, the mountain was full of horses and chariots of fire all around Elisha." (2 Kings 6:15-17 ESV)*

This story shows that spiritual forces, whether heavenly (as in the passage above) or satanic (think flaming arrows), may be surrounding us at any given time. Elisha had an accurate perception of reality. He could see what the servant could not. What did it take to change the servant's perception? The Lord answered Elisha's prayer and opened his eyes so that he could see.

The Apostle Paul, writing to the Ephesians, revealed the reality of a spiritual battle that is ever-present.

> *"For we do not wrestle against flesh and blood, but against the rulers, against the authorities, against the cosmic powers over this present darkness, against the spiritual forces of evil in the heavenly places." (Ephesians 6:12 ESV)*

Jesus stressed the permanence of the spiritual reality when He said, "For what does it profit a man to gain the whole world and forfeit his soul?" (Mark 8:36 ESV). The physical world is in the process of passing away. It does no good to prosper in the physical and yet fail in the spiritual matters of life.

It is a work of God to open our eyes and sharpen our senses to perceive the things that are real in this life and beyond. I will paraphrase A. W. Tozer from *The Pursuit of God:* We have faculties to understand the physical world and the spiritual world. Until a regenerate work is done by the Holy Spirit, our spiritual faculties lay dead, waiting to be brought to life. Even after receiving salvation, the Christian must learn to fine tune and hone his spiritual acumen by spending time in communion with God. We have tools for perception, given by God to those who believe, we just have to wake up and use them.

So then, perception *is not* reality, reality *is* reality. Jesus Christ is reality. Our spiritual lives are a reality, and we are in a spiritual life and death battle. We must pray, asking God that He would enable us to see it more clearly.

Reflection

❶ What makes it most difficult for us to see the spiritual reality?

❷ How would your life change if you saw the way Elisha did?

❸ If the spiritual is real, why do we avoid talking about it?

9

GOD OF THE GAPS

CHRISTIANS ARE SOMETIMES accused of using God to fill any gap in our understanding of how the world works. If there is a phenomenon in nature that we don't understand, skeptics would claim that we simply insert God as the explanation rather than seeking "scientific" answers. They see it as a cop-out, more or less, that allows Christians to insert the Sunday school answer of God or Jesus for virtually any question. The assertion is that as scientific discoveries or even philosophical reasoning become more advanced, there are fewer gaps and thus less of a need for God in our lives.

There is a fundamental flaw in this idea. Understanding a process or phenomenon through scientific exploration and discovery does not eliminate the need for God. Just because one understands the design does not mean one can discount the designer. That would be like saying that because we can explain the design of a car in detail, no one designed or made it. That's nonsense. The truth is, the more science reveals about the complexity of life, the stronger the case becomes for a designer! Discovery does not eliminate God but rather points to God!

"....He upholds the universe by the word of his power."
(Hebrews 1:3 ESV)

I do believe in the "God of the Gaps." He just happens to be the God of everything else as well. God has revealed Himself through the design of the universe and is therefore over all we have discovered through scientific efforts. He is also over all the areas of life that we do not understand, some of which may be open to discovery in the future. I believe God has created us with the ability to discover, not so we would deny Him, but so we would be drawn to Him as we enjoy the wonder of His creative works!

"And he is before all things, and in him all things hold together." (Colossians 1:17 ESV)

Nature is Not Natural

The sun fades, the leaves fall
   Days darken, as winter calls
      Those with wings, take to air
         Inherent navigation, leads them there

Snowflakes flurry, right on time
   Each formation, one of a kind
      Spring breaks, melting ice
         Seeds erupt, bringing life

A special home, caterpillars hide
    Weeks later, butterflies arrive
        Archer fish, capture prey
            Adjust sight, from underwater display

Tides obey, heed the command
    Before the moon, rising to stand
        Stars illumine, sky at night
            Millions of miles, still sending light

The chest expands, fills with air
    Containing life, inside it there
        An eye sees, by light refracting
            Technical design, details exacting

The heart beats, its rhythm set
    Sustaining the one, life we get
        All we observe, who put it there?
            Laws set in motion, why and from where?

Each pattern, crafted in care
    A master plan, evident there
        On its own, the ordinary
            A closer look, extraordinary

The Director, a symphony to orchestrate
    Nature's laws, an official mandate
        This nature, anything but natural
            God not imagined, but actual

Reflection

❶ Is science eliminating our need for God?

❷ What is the primary reason we need God?

❸ What does your view of nature reveal about your worldview?

10

IF A MAN WAS GOD

If a Man was God

If a man was God he'd come in great power,
  A magnificent miraculous display.
    Anxious to conquer watching enemies cower,
      Silencing scoffers and making them pay.

When God was a man he put off His great power,
  Humbling Himself as a poor baby born.
    Not conquering, but loving, until finally His hour,
      Silent before scoffers, while wearing the thorns.

If a man was God he'd gather up wealth,
  Using influence and fame to make himself known.
    Drawing the most important to himself,
      While leaving the poor and weak alone.

When God was a man He lived a peasant's life,
A wanderer who had no place to call home.
The sinners and outcasts were drawn to His side,
They were all welcomed as one of His own.

If a man was God he'd lift himself high,
Unwilling to mix with criminals shame.
Safely above, as if in the sky,
He would be careful to protect his good name.

When God was a man He was lifted up,
Like a criminal He was sentenced to die.
Drinking the wrath poured into His cup,
Enduring the shame as His accusers stood by.

If a man was God he would disown the prodigal son,
Leaving the rebel to wallow in sorrow.
The reward only to the favored one,
Leaving the guilty no hope for tomorrow.

When God was a man He sought out the lost,
Forgiving all those who knew they were broken.
Eternal rewards given at great cost,
To all those who in faith had spoken.

There is no man who will ever be God,
But there is a God who stooped to be man.
Jesus is the one man who is rightly called God,
And He's also the God who became that one
man

Reflection

❶ Why is God's approach so vastly different from our own?

❷ If you were God, what would you do differently? How would the world be different?

❸ Think back through history. How do the most powerful individuals behave?

11

I BELIEVE IN GOD, BUT ...

MY FIRST COLLEGE religion class left a lasting impression on me. I remember being very curious as I enrolled in "Old Testament Survey," a required course for earning a degree at my school. The professor was familiar to me; he attended the same church I did in our small college town. If I recall correctly he even filled the pulpit occasionally when our pastor was absent. This course was to be the first formal religious instruction I would receive outside church and my parents' teaching at home.

During the first few weeks of class, I became very uncomfortable as the professor presented a view of Scripture that saw it filled with allegories instead of actualities. A literal six-day creation became just a symbolic picture of God's relationship to humans. Noah's ark and the worldwide flood became a local phenomenon. Jonah was cast as a fictional character rather than a historical person. The date of the prophetic writings were questioned as was the authorship of many of the Old Testament books. Needless to say I was disappointed greatly. My frustration remains to this day over the low view of Scripture presented to hundreds of college students at my alma mater, which was purported to be a Christian college.

It has been well over a decade since I completed "Old Testament Survey," but I still have nagging questions that remain unanswered. Is it possible to have too much faith in God's Word? Should we believe the events recorded in scripture literally, or is that for the uneducated, the unsophisticated, and the naïve? When does our belief in God go too far? I fear that many "believers" accept God and even the sacrificial work of Jesus on the cross, but when it comes to issues such as creation, Noah's ark, Jonah, or the parting of the Red Sea, we shrug with some hesitation. It seems there are some stories that are just too incredible to actually believe.

Where does this hesitation come from? Does this show an erosion of faith? One of the causal factors for new interpretations of God's Word is what I will call *reconciliation*. This is not the kind of reconciling that occurs when two friends settle a disagreement. This is the idea that we can make the revelation of God congruent with the knowledge of man. (We make God's revelation in the image of our own human understanding, not the other way around.).

Some Christians attempt to reconcile modern scientific theory with biblical teaching. For example, the promotion of evolutionary theory has caused some to abandon a literal six-day creation in attempts to conform God's Word to man's understanding. Theories are invented to somehow mesh what secular science tells us is true with what God tells us is true. Science would teach us that miracles are an impossible violation of the laws of nature, and therefore the stories of Jonah and Noah have to be interpreted allegorically.

Scholars at distinguished universities tell us that the Bible is mere literature written by fallible human beings and thus has no unique status as the Word of God. Entire books have been written (and become quite popular) for the sole purpose of undermining the credibility of Scripture. Groups such as "The Jesus Seminar" have had their influence on mainstream thought as well. This degraded view of the Bible has crept into the church and in some cases is subtle and in others it is glaring. Trying to reconcile modern liberal scholarship with what the Bible actually says has devastating results. It dilutes and devalues the message God conveys through his Word. What does God say when it comes to the wisdom of man?

> *"...and the wisdom of their wise men shall perish, and the discernment of their discerning men shall be hidden." (Isaiah 29:14 ESV)*

> *"For the word of the cross is folly to those who are perishing, but to us who are being saved it is the power of God. For it is written, 'I will destroy the wisdom of the wise, and the discernment of the discerning I will thwart.'" Where is the one who is wise? Where is the scribe? Where is the debater of this age? Has not God made foolish the wisdom of the world?" (1 Corinthians 1:18-20 ESV)*

> *"...but they became futile in their thinking, and their foolish hearts were darkened. Claiming to be wise, they became fools." (Romans 1:21-22 ESV)*

The eternal Word of God has no need to be reconciled to the wisdom of man. It stands alone pure and true and trustworthy.

As troublesome as the concept of reconciliation is, what is more frustrating is that many of the people advancing these ideas claim to believe in God but then add a qualifier to their belief. "I believe in God ... *but*." I find this quite fascinating and incredibly inconsistent. It is inconceivable how one can say "I believe in God" but then deny miracles.

"I believe in God, but the story of Jonah and the big fish is simply too much to swallow" (pun intended).

"I believe in God, but the flood could not have been worldwide; that is just too incredible."

"I believe in God, but the creation story does not fit what I read in my science textbook." Isn't there an obvious disconnect here? Once you allow for God, anything is possible! The fact that you and I exist is a miracle that God performed. We cannot put a regulator on God. Why do we seek to limit Him? Doesn't belief in God automatically give Him the benefit of *any* doubt? We do not have the liberty to define God. He is self-defining. It is my opinion that you cannot *sort of* believe in God. You either do or you do not. Partial belief isn't really belief at all.

One day I will stand before God Almighty. May it be said of me that I believed too much instead of too little. If I am wrong about a literal six-day creation and other miracles recorded in Scripture so be it, but I would rather have God say "Son, your faith was too great" than "Why did you doubt me?" When it comes to God (and it always does), I will err on the side of trust every time.

Reflection

❶ Are there different classes of believers – some sophisticated and some naïve?

❷ Isn't sharing our Christian faith easier if we downplay the incredible events recorded in the Bible?

❸ Do you struggle to believe certain miraculous events in the Bible?

12

WHAT IS GOD LIKE?

What is God Like?

What is God like,
   Has He made Himself known?
      Searching to find Him,
         And become one of His own.

Who can equal God's great power,
   Or the days that He has spanned?
      Who has taught Him anything,
         Or known the work of His hands?

God is the great Creator,
   His goodness pleased to share.
      Always in relationship,
         The Trinity forever there.

God eternally incomprehensible,
    The Father, Spirit, and Son.
      What a wonderful mystery,
        The Godhead three, and yet one.

God is not like me,
    His love is constant and strong,
      When I often stumble,
        God shows His suffering long.

When in sin I turned my back,
    Death, the wages mine.
      God did the unthinkable,
        Becoming man, born into time.

While on earth no glory found,
    Humility personified.
      Suffered at the hands of men,
        And for my sins He died.

The grave could not hold Him,
    On the third day He rose.
      Defeated the enemy,
        Bringing death's reign to close.

No one could have imagined,
    The Almighty of creation,
      Showing Himself to sinful people,
        Through Jesus' revelation.

Seeking those who hated him,
    Spitting in His face.
      Overcoming evil with good,
        Through endless love and grace.

Too grand to be invented,
   Beyond the thought of man.
      Who could see this kind of God,
         Or the redemption He had planned?

So what is God like?
   What can possibly compare?
      There is nothing like Him,
         It would be like grasping for air.

I ponder in meditation,
   The God who makes Himself known.
      Loving hostile souls,
         And making them His own.

Reflection

❶ What would God look like if people had invented Him?

❷ In what way is God most unlike human beings?

❸ If this is a true portrayal of God, are you drawn to Him?

13

THE INTELLIGENCE BEHIND DESIGN

The Intelligence Behind Design

Cars evolved from bicycles you know.
  Both have wheels that make them go,
    Both take people to and fro,
      Perhaps from a bike a car did grow.

A bike is just a car that's small,
  A simpler form of machine that's all.
    Both have horns that ring and call,
      Cars may crash and bikes may fall.

Each has pedals for your feet,
  And brakes to stop while on the street.
    Most come with adjustable seats,
      This close relation is hard to beat.

Less complex with smaller gears,
  But like a car, a wheel to steer.
    A bicycle given millions of years,
      And surely then the car appears.

The car's precursor is finally found,
  An ancient relative that rolls on the ground.
    Making its way in the journal rounds,
      Celebrating a discovery so profound.

Can a car rise out of natural selection,
  Evolving through time to almost perfection?
    At this point I must raise an objection,
      This picture needs some closer inspection!

Similarities always point to a plan,
  Leading back to a designer's hand.
    Both are inventions from the mind of man,
      This obvious truth is where I stand!

Looking in this world you will find,
  Many creatures, each after its kind.
    Not some random process of time,
      No, but a Creator's great design.

Reflection

❶ How do you explain the design of life?

❷ Does design require a designer?

❸ How does worldview affect the way we interpret apparent

- 14 -

ABOUT MIRACLES

"The principle problem for the atheist is that he exists."

IT IS ALWAYS interesting to think about the miraculous. Any unique event that defies the laws of nature and is totally against what our everyday experience has been is certainly worth some attention. Some of the most celebrated arguments against Christianity have been based on the denial of miracles. I heard one of these arguments recently while watching a debate about the Resurrection. The critic claimed that the primary function of historians is to determine what *probably* happened in the past. None of us was there to witness ancient history, so we are merely piecing together a puzzle based upon probability. The argument against miracles goes something like this: Since, by definition, miracles are extraordinarily rare and improbable, they are the least probable explanation for any historical event. Therefore, a good historian can never say that a miracle occurred in the past, especially the distant past, because he/she should never use the least *probable* explanation in trying to determine what *probably* happened.

On the surface, this argument sounds good. It is clever, if nothing else. There are several problems, however, not the least of which is the blindfolding of the historian before the investigation ever begins. Using the probability rule exempts the critic from the consideration of all possible explanations because no matter how weighty the evidence, miracles are off the table. This is entering the investigation with a closed mind. It also provides an "out" if no other obvious explanation other than the miraculous makes sense. In the case of the Resurrection, the "historian" can throw his arms in the air and say, "I don't know what happened, but I know it wasn't a miracle."

Consider this idea from a different angle. What if the probability rule was applied to the origin of the universe or the origin of life on our planet? By astronomical odds, the least probable event ever is the random forming a universe that supports life. If we use the probability rule, we do not exist! The rule fails because we do exist. The highly improbable is the reality. The same is true for the Resurrection. The fact is that we have an empty tomb. Jesus is not in it. The highly improbable is the reality. It is the reality that we need to consider, not focusing on clever arguments based on semantics, and not starting with presuppositions that limit conclusions, which is itself unscientific (for the scientific method bases conclusions on observation not presuppositions, right?).

What about those who say the Bible is not true because it contains miracles? This is a common blunder in the criticism of Christianity. Argue against the theories of aerodynamics, not against airplanes. Argue against the reflection of light, not against your face in the mirror. Argue against the existence of God, but not against His work. Once airplanes are flying, you see your own face, and miracles are documented, the train has left the station and you missed it. Or put another way: It is easier to doubt the existence of the Mississippi River when you are not standing on its banks. By all accounts, based on probability, we should not be here – which means that each one of us is a miracle! Arguing against miracles is undermining the very ground on which you stand. The principle problem for the atheist is that he exists.

Some try to discredit the events in the Bible as impossible because they are so extraordinary and contrary to anything we have ever observed in nature. Thus, the argument goes, they could never have happened the way the Bible describes. This criticism arises from a naturalistic viewpoint. The Creation, the Flood, and Christ's Resurrection are not natural events. Therefore, they cannot be explained by natural causes. Of course, Noah couldn't build a boat, just as something cannot come from nothing and as dead people don't rise again.

For the skeptic to claim that it would have been too difficult to care for the animals on the ark, or that the boat would have sunk, is to exclude the hand of God from the equation. If God is not working, the skeptic is correct. These events seem like a miraculous departure from the laws of nature, and indeed they are. When we consider the origin of logic, reason, consciousness, scientific laws, the universe, and life itself, we are dealing in the stuff of miracles as none of these things could have spontaneously erupted from nothingness. That means all scientific discovery finds its roots in the miraculous.

Once you allow for God, anything is possible. Frankly, the miracles themselves are not what Christianity is all about. The miracles serve to point us to an amazing God who cares enough about us to make Himself known through the improbable, impossible, and miraculous.

Reflection

❶ Why are we so hesitant to consider miracles?

❷ If there is a God, should it be difficult to believe in the miraculous?

❸ In the Bible, how did those who witnessed a miracle typically respond?

15

OLD EARTH RIPPLES

"Old earth creationism seeks to provide scientific answers, but it leads to new theological questions."

A DEBATE IS PRESENT within the church today regarding the age of the universe. Simply put, some Christians believe the universe is young and others believe it is old. Those who take the latter position are known as old earth creationists. There are several variants of old earth creation theory, but all share a belief of progressive creation over billions of years. All old earth proponents would hold that death was present prior to the entrance of sin into the world, which Scripture tells us was the result from Adam's fall. Old earth creationism has gained traction because it fits with age of the earth theorized by most modern scientists. Some would say old earth creationism is a blending of scientific truth with biblical truth.

In evaluating this theory, we must ask what effects these ideas are having on the interpretation and overall view of God's Word?

Just as you cannot throw a stone into water without causing a ripple, so you cannot move the foundation of a house without shifting the entire structure. I do not know how old the earth is. I am not a trained theologian or scientist. What I do know is that accepting an old earth framework causes a ripple effect through the rest of Scripture that anyone espousing this position must consider and address.

The primary question I want to consider is why? What would motivate us as Christians to change long-held interpretations of God's Word? The answer is simple: Science. More specifically, modern scientific theory regarding the age of the earth and the origins of humans.

The following sections discuss just a few examples of the ripples that move through Scripture as a whole because of old earth ideology.

What is a day? New interpretations of old words

Books have been written on this topic. All scholars agree that the Hebrew word for day can be used in different ways. Exodus 20:11, however, puts this issue to rest for me. God's people were to structure their work week according the template God followed during the week of creation. I like my job, but I do not want to work for *ages* waiting for the weekend! Right or wrong, there is no doubt that new interpretations of these passages have been promoted by old earth creationists.

Where and how did Adam and Eve live?

The answer to this question may vary depending on the flavor of progressive creation one prefers, but all would agree that Adam and Eve did not live in a Sunday school version of the Garden of Eden. If Adam and Eve were created during the final stage of creation, then they entered into a very hostile world. It would be akin to dropping an unsuspecting newlywed couple in the remote Amazon jungle and asking them to fend for themselves. We could speculate that God cordoned off a small section of creation and supernaturally maintained a paradise there, but I think this idea could raise more questions than it answers. What happens if Adam had obeyed God and the Fall did not occur? It doesn't seem consistent to have the entire universe in a state of decay while the Garden remains untouched. This is certainly a ripple effect and not part of traditional interpretations.

Have your cake and eat it, too

To maintain some semblance of the doctrine of original sin, some old earth creationists believe in a literal Adam and Eve. If they do not, their position simply becomes theistic evolution, which is even more difficult to reconcile with salvation doctrine and easier to criticize scientifically because of the problems with the theory of evolution. This is a very fine line to walk. On one side we have an allegorical interpretation of the creation account, but on the other we must find a way somehow to preserver a literal Adam and Eve. This seems like an unnecessary balancing act.

Does the Flood account need to be reinterpreted?

The short answer is *Yes*. The Noahic Flood is seen as an allegory or a local event. Perhaps not all old earth adherents hold this view, but the theory leaves the door open. I am not a geologist, but it is my impression that accepting billions of years of geologic change AND accepting a worldwide flood at this same time is inconsistent or possibly incompatible. At any rate, old earth interpretation casts doubt on the worldwide flood. This, once more, is a rereading of Scripture tailored to fit an old earth view.

Death before the Fall?

I see this as the greatest problem for old earth creationism. For the old earth position to work scripturally we must go throughout the New Testament and reinterpret the meaning of the words death, world, creation, futility, corruption, and many others. See Romans 5:12-14 and Romans 8:18-21. What is the basis for this new interpretation? It is the attempt to reconcile God's Word with what modern science tells us is the age of the earth. I do not believe any alternate interpretations of these passages were common prior to our "enlightenment" by modern science. Conservative interpretation says that death, both biological and spiritual, entered the universe because of Adam's sin. For old earth ideas to work, this has to be changed. Ultimately, this impacts the understanding of what Christ accomplished in the shedding of His blood for our sins.

A new heaven and a new earth – animals finally catch a break

According to progressive creation, millions of animals perished prior to Adam and Eve's showing up on the scene. Many of them were eaten. We encounter a problem, however, when the Bible speaks about the restoration of creation and the wolf lying down with the lamb. Old Earth believers posit that animals will be provided a new level of glorification and will no longer be carnivorous at that point. The idea of restoring what was originally "good" about creation has to be altered.

Science and miracles

Secular scientists exclude the possibility of miracles based upon the fixed laws of nature. Unlike the conclusions of historical or forensic science, the conclusions drawn against miracles can be tested and observed, making the case even stronger. The observational evidence says that miracles do not happen, *period*. Because of this strong scientific finding perhaps we should deny the miracles recorded in the New Testament. Should the New Testament be reinterpreted in light of the science? The slope is starting to feel a little slippery.

Is God really good? Does He create that which is good?
Christians rely on a good God creating a good world to answer questions about suffering and evil. We suffer because of sin that entered and corrupted God's perfect creation. The idea that God created a flawed world that included decay, death, and suffering (even if it was not human) degrades that argument. In fact, it makes God the author and creator not only of the "good" but also of decay, death, suffering, and perhaps evil (which is heresy). If I were an atheist, I would pounce on this one.

Conclusion
Perhaps old earth creationism is correct. If so, however, it requires some dramatic changes to the way we view and interpret Scripture. It sends a ripple, or maybe a tidal wave, throughout the rest of Scripture. I would argue it requires us to rethink our concept of God altogether.

I challenge all old earth creationists to ask themselves a serious questions: *Why? Why do I believe this is true? Does the answer come from inside or from outside the Word of God? Do I consider science to be on the same level as scripture?*

Reflection

❶ Why has science achieved a level of unquestioned authority when the Word of God is becoming increasingly marginalized?

❷ Are young earth creation proponents placing a stumbling block in front of potential believers?

❸ Is it possible to be scientific and still believe the Bible?

16

CURING CANCER

*"Avoiding death in this life is less important
than seeking life after death."*

I WAS READING ON a web site that claimed to have proof that God is a fabrication of the human mind. Several of the "proofs" presented criticized the seemingly ineffective prayer lives of Christian believers. Jesus directed His followers to pray and said their prayers would be answered if asked in His name. So the critic questions what would happen if believers prayed sincerely for all cancer in the world to be cured. The conclusion is that the great collective prayer in Jesus' name would go unanswered and that therefore Jesus is a liar. If Jesus is a liar, God is imaginary.

This made me think "What if God did cure all the cancer in the world?" It would no doubt end suffering and potential premature death for millions of people. Devastated parents would have children restored to health, an anxious wife would feel secure having her husband healed, and friends would no longer grieve over the loss of someone close. It would be a glad day to be sure! But step back for a moment and look at the bigger picture. All of those people whose cancer was healed would eventually succumb to the death that is ever-present in our world. Some would have tragic accidents, others may contract a lethal virus or bacteria, and many would develop heart disease and other ailments common to an aging population. Some would no doubt live long lives and then die of so-called "natural" causes. Many of those who were healed would suffer relational strife, grief over the loss of friends and loved ones, financial difficulties, and the general stress of just living. Let's face it, even at its best, this life can be trying.

Consider a real-life example. The smallpox virus was a devastating cause of disease, suffering, and death. Thanks to vaccination programs, this deadly virus is now essentially eradicated. This advancement has greatly improved the quality of life for millions of people around the world. But has it improved the quality of the *after*life? What has the end of this disease done for spiritual health? Our temporal, physical lives are improved, but our eternal, spiritual lives are unchanged. Those who were spared smallpox will live on to face other, sometimes even greater, challenges.

What happened to all the people Jesus healed miraculously during His three-year ministry on earth? As far as we know, *all of them died*. Some probably died believing in Jesus and others perhaps grew bitter against Him because He did not meet their messianic expectations of a conquering king. Looking back from our perspective today, the physical healing now pales in comparison to the spiritual healing. If they missed out on the spiritual, the physical matters very little at this point – and throughout eternity.

Dying is a bad thing, but I would argue that it is not the *worst* thing. The curing of disease is a great thing, but I would argue that it is not the *best* thing. Avoiding death in this life is less important than seeking life after death.

Unless every malady known to humans were eliminated and we were given eternal life living in flawless bodies, the curing of cancer or any other disease is simply trading one cause of suffering for another. It just puts off the inevitable. So, then, it makes sense to us what God would do (if He was really God) is to give us flawless bodies in a world free of disease and death where life would be eternally sweet.

Perhaps God sees something that is not always obvious to us. This is the fact that life is but a "mist that appears for a little while and then vanishes" (James 4:14). Life on earth is short; eternity is very long. The healing of our physical bodies is temporarily good but ultimately worthless if we forfeit our souls. God's desire is the healing of our bodies, but not just our bodies. The problem we face is this: We die not because our *bodies* are broken but because our *spirits* are broken. We are separated from God by our own doing, and by definition this brings death. God *is* life and the Creator and sustainer of all things, so to be separate from Him is to dwell in darkness, decay, and death. The only way God can heal us physically is to first bring our spirits back to life. Fortunately God has a plan to fix our problem:

> *"For God so loved the world, that he gave his only Son, that whoever believes in him should not perish but have eternal life." (John 3:16 ESV)*

It is interesting to note here that God had a plan of absolute (not temporary) salvation in place before any human prayer had ever been uttered.

So God does have a plan to give us flawless bodies in a world free of disease and death where life will be eternally sweet. Sometimes I think we created beings think too small. It is easy to shake a fist at God, angry that He will not answer every prayer to cure a temporary disease such as cancer. We miss the point, which is that God is making *all* things new by curing us of our eternal deadness through Jesus. He is preparing an eternal home for us. He is just waiting for us to accept His offer of salvation.

Thank you, Father, that in Your wisdom You do not give us what we think we want but rather provide for us exactly what we need by making us new through Your Son, Jesus. *Amen.*

Reflection

❶ How do we balance our desire for *physical* health with our desire for *spiritual* health?

❷ If we had no physical ailments, would we draw closer to, or farther from, God?

❸ When are you most likely to call out for God's help?

17

POWER WITHOUT PERSONALITY

"The Cosmos is all that is or was or ever will be."
– Carl Sagan

"I am the Alpha and the Omega, the first and the last,
the beginning and the end."
– Jesus Christ

WHAT WOULD YOU think I was referring to if I described a force that has incredible power, transcends time, formed the universe, created the earth, brought forth life, and will one day bring everything to an end? What is the first thought that comes into your mind? Now, what if I told you that atheists believe in this force?

What if I told you about a great power that is not observable but is thought to be present and holding everything in the universe together? Now what if I told you that modern secular science promotes this power?

To account for some unexplainable phenomena in the universe (including where it came from) scientists are looking in some interesting directions. They have theorized an energy that holds our universe together but is unseen and to this point not subject to scientific testing. It is called "dark energy," and it works alongside another mysterious entity called "dark matter."

There is a growing theory regarding the origin and supposed privileged status of our habitable universe. It is called the "multiverse." According to this idea, there are an infinite number of alternate universes parallel to our own. Somewhere there is a universe "factory" that is producing these worlds. Because there are billions upon billions of universes out there, ours is not really so unique after all.

Scientists develop these theories because, without them, things just don't add up the way they should. Something is missing. There seem to be factors working behind the scenes that are just beyond our reach. Attempting to explain each theory in detail is beyond the scope and purpose of this chapter.

The point is that scientists are looking to the unseen, the unknown, and the eternal, and bestowing these qualities upon nature. This is a deification of the natural realm. By deification, I mean attributing to nature the characteristics typically reserved for God, including great power, creativity, and infinitude. There is great power in the invisible energy that supposedly holds sway over the fate of the universe. There is awesome creative force in a process that can generate billions of universes including our own wonderfully designed home. And since something cannot come from nothing, these forces are thought to be eternally present, demonstrating infinitude. A community that in large part is made up of agnostics and atheists is showing a stunning degree of faith. Could it be that atheists actually believe in God after all?

I found some definitions of God in the Merriam-Webster Dictionary and altered them slightly for illustration.

God:

1. The supreme or ultimate reality.
2. Something credited for the creation of the universe.
3. One controlling a particular aspect or part of reality.
4. Something that has great power, strength, knowledge, etc., and that can affect nature and the lives of people.

Each of these definitions fits well into the framework of the aforementioned theories. But what is missing? *Personality*. It appears that an atheist will indeed believe in God (as defined in the dictionary) as long as personality is removed. That is, they accept it as long as it is a sterile, non-relational, amoral force rather than a personal force. So it is not the power, or transcendence, or even the creativity that they shun but rather the person. For the atheist, the problem is not a lack of faith; it is a lack of *personal* faith.

Compare the definitions above to the dictionary definitions where the person of God is emphasized:

1. The perfect and all powerful *Spirit* or *Being* . . . who created and rules the universe.
2. The *Being* perfect in power, wisdom, and goodness, who is worshipped as creator and ruler of the universe.
3. A *Being* . . . controlling a particular aspect or part of reality.
4. A *Being* that has great power, strength, knowledge, etc., and that can affect nature and the lives of people.

They reject or suppress the personal God because along with the personality comes relationship. If God is a person, then we are in relationship to Him. Being in relationship means we are accountable for our side of the relationship. Ultimately, we answer to God as our authority instead of to ourselves. This is an uncomfortable scenario for us, which we can remedy easily by simply removing God's personality from the equation.

In some ways, the idea of God cannot be avoided. We will either accept a personal God who created nature or an impersonal god that is nature itself. We will either worship the Creator or the creation. In a sense, we all believe in a great power that is over us – even a great power that created us. Christians believe that power has a personality, who is motivated by love and is intricately involved in our lives. Atheists believe in the power without the personality, thereby avoiding the relationship and the responsibility that comes with it.

". . . He upholds the universe by the word of his power." (Hebrews 1:3 ESV)

Reflection

❶ Why do we fight so hard against a personal God?

❷ Is it a question of authority?

❸ Could science be considered a god to some?

18

PERSPECTIVE ON TRIALS

GOD HAS AN eternal perspective. He is more concerned about our eternal and spiritual wellbeing than our temporal and physical wellbeing. An example of this is Jesus' first forgiving a lame man's sins and then, almost as an afterthought, healing his body. Which is more important, forgiveness of sins (resulting in eternal life) or healing of the body (which will eventually die)? "What does it profit a man to gain the whole world and forfeit his soul?" Jesus asked.

We tend to focus on our current physical circumstances and events which, when they are favorable, can lull us into self-reliance and false confidence and when unfavorable, sometimes leave us questioning if God is really in control, or if God cares for us, or in some cases questioning whether God exists at all.

Hardship can have two general effects: (1) it can draw us closer to God because we see our helplessness, or (2) cause us to reject God because we question His goodness. We either shake an angry fist at God because of the pain in our circumstance or bow a humble knee before Him in submission to His will. Comfort, on the other hand, nearly always causes us forgetful people to take our eyes off of God and look to ourselves or some other object (money or accomplishment perhaps) for our security and wellbeing. How quick we are to take credit for the good in our lives and take our seat firmly on the throne of self-determination, forgetting that we cannot even make our own heart beat.

What if God, who is all-knowing, loving, and wise, brings hardship into our lives knowing that if our faith is strong we can be a light for Him and an example of the strength He brings or that if we lack faith or have no faith at all we may be nudged to look to God for salvation? After all, if God fixes all our circumstances to our liking – whether physical health, work issues, wealth, security, or other material possessions we need/want – then all these things will pass away in the end. But if we endure hardship and grow spiritually or meet Jesus for the first time or show a lost person the way, is this not much better eternally (James 1:2-4)? Remember that God has eternity in mind. He sees clearly what we often forget, namely that although this life on earth is short what happens here will punch the ticket for our eternal destiny.

This is not to say that God does not care about our physical lives or circumstances. Of course God knows that we have physical needs and desires in life, and He often generously provides for us (Matthew 6:25-33). The point is that in certain situations His allowing us to face trials can benefit us and, sometimes even more powerfully, benefit those who are watching us by pointing them to the source of our strength, Jesus Christ!

We need to remember that this world is not right. It is broken and cursed and not as God intended. This world will never bring us satisfaction or security. Even when our own personal lives are going well, our neighbor across the street or across the world may be suffering immensely. Ours is a world in which we humans have tried to take the reins and control our own lives. We have told ourselves that we do not need God. We have rebelled against the presence of God and are separated from Him. Therefore, **suffering and tragedy are rampant in this place**. But God is not willing to see us left to our own devices and perish. He has a plan for rescue (John 3:16). God Himself became a man we call Jesus, who infiltrated this fallen world, came behind enemy lines, and won the battle over sin and death by His perfect life, crucifixion, and, most importantly, His resurrection. He now offers to *rescue us from this place* and give us a home with Him for eternity. What does He ask from us in return? Just that we believe. Believe that what He did was enough, that there is nothing that needs to be or could be added to the work of Jesus. Believe that we are helpless in ourselves and have nothing to offer for our own rescue except to receive the free gift.

This is a broken world, and we should not expect life here to be easy, even as Christians (Jesus promised us difficulty in John 16:33). It has been said that "life would not be so hard if we didn't expect it to be so easy." Again, this is a matter of perspective. If we seek ease, comfort, and satisfaction in this world, we will be disappointed every time. Our wealth and accomplishments fade and our physical bodies decay. If we seek eternal satisfaction and set our minds on the things above, we will not be disappointed, and the trials we face today will seem as "light afflictions" compared to eternal glory (Romans 8:18; 2 Corinthians 4:17).

Reflection

❶ What are our expectations in life?

❷ What do we do when reality differs from our expectations?

- 19 -

THINGS UNSEEN

Things Unseen

My hope is placed in things unseen,
   Nothing in this world compares.
      So temporal is a treasure's gleam,
         A home for me the Lord prepares.

Walking by faith not by sight,
   By the abundance of Your grace.
      My heart opened so I might,
         Finally see Your face.

But my flesh is so weak,
   And it is wasting away.
      When God alone I seek,
         My spirit renews each day.

As Peter faltered on the raging sea,
I lose my focus and start to stray.
My earthly eyes so often deceive,
O my God, please show the way.

Looking forward to what will be,
The things of this world fade away.
Prepare me for eternal glory,
These light afflictions of today.

Something will last through all eternity,
Onto what will you fix your grasp?
There is more to hold than what we see,
Only what is God's will last.

No accomplishment will stand,
This is truth for every human being.
No possession held in hand,
None will last but the things unseen.

"So we do not lose heart. Though our outer self is wasting away, our inner self is being renewed day by day. For this light momentary affliction is preparing for us an eternal weight of glory beyond all comparison, as we look not to the things that are seen but to the things that are unseen. For the things that are seen are transient, but the things that are unseen are eternal." (2 Corinthians 4:16-18 ESV)

Reflection

❶ Which is easier – to trust in material things or to trust in God?

❷ Why are we so easily lured into hoping for things we know will fail us?

❸ What will be the lasting legacy of your life?

– 20 –

CIRCUMSTANTIAL EVIDENCE

THIS LEGAL TERM is familiar to us today thanks to television series such as "Law & Order" and "CSI." Anyone who has watched these shows can recall an episode in which a witness is on the stand providing testimony when the defense attorney stands up and shouts, "Objection, your honor, that is circumstantial!" To which the judge replies with either a "sustained" or an "overruled" pronouncement and the trial continues.

Investigating the circumstances surrounding an event, such as a crime, can be helpful in determining what actually took place. By definition, however, circumstantial evidence leaves the door open to more than one possible explanation. For example, let's consider a common crime committed in my household – toddler vandalism. The victim is a recently painted white door in our home, which now has red marker scribbles up to a height of about four feet. The suspect is a three-year-old boy with red marker streaks on his arms and face. These circumstances would suggest that the boy is guilty of the crime.

But is there any other possible explanation? Is it possible that his artful big sister colored on the door, which appeared to her to be a beautiful, clean white canvas and then turned her red markers on her little brother and decorated him shortly thereafter? Or maybe a friend came over and became overzealous during coloring time. You can see that the circumstantial evidence in this case seems to point strongly to one conclusion and yet there are other conclusions that are just as viable and need to be considered.

In life, many people look at their circumstances and then make a judgment about God. For example, someone may say, "There is so much suffering in the world that God must not exist." Another may say, "My life is such a mess. Why is God punishing me? I don't deserve this." These are valid complaints. It could be that God is punishing some people, or that maybe He doesn't exist, but does the evidence leave the possibility of any other explanations?

While reading the book of the prophet Amos recently, a certain passage struck me. In a time of prosperity, the people of Israel had grown complacent and comfortable and turned away from God and toward pagan idolatry. God intervened by changing their prosperity into hardship. The Lord, speaking through Amos in chapter 4:6-11, stated that He withheld food and rain, struck down crops, sent locusts and pestilence, killed the young men with the sword, and carried away their wealth. These circumstances could be interpreted in many different ways. Was God being vindictive? Had He abandoned the people altogether? A refrain used five times in this passage reveals the heart of God: "Yet you did not return to me."

God was bringing these difficulties upon them in His desperation to save this rebellious people. His purpose was born out of love. But the people remained stubborn in their ways and were eventually conquered by the invading Assyrian army. This passage struck me because it showed that even in severe tribulation and what must have seemed like random natural disaster, God was working to draw His people back into a right relationship.

Consider other examples from scripture, such as the life of Joseph in the book of Genesis. Joseph went through many trials and hardships without having the benefit of knowing how the story would end. It turns out that God used Joseph's life mightily to rescue his entire family and preserve the nation of Israel. During these times, Joseph rightly judged the circumstantial evidence as being from God and remained faithful in all that he did. What about the Apostle Paul? In 2 Corinthians 11:23-28 he described the multiple trials he endured, all while working as a faithful servant of Christ. Did Paul lament that God was cursing him? No. The purpose was made clear in 2 Corinthians 12:10:

"For the sake of Christ, then, I am content with weaknesses, insults, hardships, persecutions, and calamities. For when I am weak, then I am strong."

Looking forward to the end times, the book of Revelation describes multiple tribulations that will occur on the earth. Revelation 9:20 says that despite these trials, the remaining people on the earth did not repent. Just as He did in the days of Amos, the Lord is using one last ditch effort to get a stubborn people's attention.

God has a purpose behind our circumstances that is not always obvious. When we examine the "circumstantial evidence" in our lives, we need to keep that in focus. As we saw in the examples above, God sometimes uses hardship to drive people to their knees in repentance. In other cases, hardship is the result of faithful service or intended to bring about a greater good. Trials are not necessarily a punishment. At times we are to see our trials as a blessing (James 1:2; Acts 5:41).

When we are enduring the trials of life and our hearts "object" to the set of circumstances we are in, we should "overrule" those objections and remember with Amos that "he who forms the mountains and creates the wind and declares to man what is his thought … the Lord, the God of hosts…" (Amos 4:13) is ultimately in control and has our eternal wellbeing in mind.

Reflection

❶ Would our perspective change if we saw life the way God does?

❷ Think of a trial you are facing now (or have faced in the past). Consider what God's purpose might be in letting you go through it?

❸ Why do we assume we are looking at the same picture God is looking at?

21

I DON'T DESERVE THIS

I Don't Deserve This

Trudging through the trials in life,
   When circumstances run amiss.
      Questioning the pain and strife,
         Why, God? I don't deserve this.

But looking at my Savior's hands,
   Pierced, along with wounded side.
      Slowly starting to understand,
         The cross on which He died.

To me He shows this endless grace,
   Willing to taste death's bitter kiss.
      Suffering the penalty in my place,
         Such love! I don't deserve **this**.

"The beauty of grace is that it makes life not fair." – Relient K.

Reflection

❶ What would happen if we actually got what we deserved?

❷ Why do we think we deserve anything at all?

❸ In an atheistic worldview, what do you deserve?

22

MAKING SENSE

"We cannot be a meaningful drop in a meaningless bucket."

EVERYONE WANTS LIFE to make sense. We all want the puzzle pieces of life to fit the picture on the box top of our imagination. When something happens that is unexpected, out of left field, unpredictable, and confusing we often complain, "That doesn't make sense!" Have you ever noticed the tendency we have for thinking that *nothing* makes sense when life is difficult but that *everything* makes sense when life is good? Too often, when something bad happens we question the order of the universe, and when something good happens we nod our head in approval because finally somebody got it right.

For example, when something really great happens in your life, how often do you say, "This just doesn't make sense, something is not right here, how could this happen?" Or perhaps in a more pointed way, "How could God let this happen?" For us selfish people, "sense" means things are going well, and "nonsense" means they are going poorly. We often miss both the blessings found in hardship and the curses found in comfort.

Maybe a better question is, "Why would life ever make sense?"

To what or to whom are we appealing when we seek to make sense of our circumstances and why do we feel entitled to some orderly progression for our lives? The making of sense is entirely a theological proposition. In fact, only the atheist can say, "Life doesn't make sense." Sense is something reserved the theist alone. The idea of making sense implies purpose or meaning, both of which are absent in an atheistic worldview. For the atheist, each day begins and ends with nonsense. The universe itself had no sense or purpose in its origins and will leave no sense or meaning upon its demise. How could there be any expectation, hope, or even a dream of life working out for our good in a Godless universe that has no overarching storyline? We cannot be a meaningful drop in a meaningless bucket.

Tragic accidents aren't tragic, unexpected fortune is not fortunate, events just occur randomly with no regard for those involved or for what they "deserved." The evil don't deserve punishment and the good don't deserve rewards. Everything is futility and in the end everyone ends up in the same place – nowhere, nothingness, and emptiness.

The atheist may respond by saying, "Any rational person observing the world we live in will conclude that life does not make sense, which is exhibit A in the case against God." However, consider a thought provoking quote from C. S. Lewis,

> "If the whole universe has no meaning, we should never
> have found out that it has no meaning: just as, if there
> were no light in the universe and therefore no creatures

with eyes, we should never know it was dark. Dark would be without meaning." – Mere Christianity

This quote has fascinated me for years. According to Lewis, even the most basic atheistic argument is taken away because inhabitants created by and living in a meaningless universe would have no capacity or ability or desire to recognize their plight. It is only because we are *created by God* as purpose driven, meaning seeking beings that we attempt to make sense of the world and our circumstances. Cavefish, which don't have eyes, spend little time searching for the light, and never complain about the dark! God has placed within us a "sense meter" which is always active and ultimately pointing us back toward Him. The fact that we make any judgment about the meaning of life, whether positive or negative, counts as evidence for God, not against God!

So what should we do when life is difficult to understand and we can't seem to determine what God has planned for us? We need to remember that for those who love God and are called according to His purpose – *all* things, both hardship and blessing, work together for our good (Romans 8:28). As demonstrated time after time in Scripture, God can use even those things which are perpetrated with evil intentions for our ultimate good and His ultimate glory. Living in this broken world is often hard, but we can take courage knowing that our lives here are temporary, God is in control, and one day we will see the "sense" of it all. In the meantime, enter into God's rest, trust Him in the good times and the bad, and understand that there is nothing that can separate us from His love.

Reflection

❶ Why do we expect life to make sense?

❷ Can suffering ever make sense?

❸ Do you agree with the statement, "If life was meaningless, we wouldn't know it"?

– 23 –

INNOCENT BY ASSOCIATION

As I was driving in my car last week I saw a bumper sticker that read "Guilty by Association." Of course, most of us have heard and used this common saying. As I followed the car with the sticker, the truth of that statement really struck home. Our identity rests on who or what we hold close. Our associations point to the state of our hearts. To what are we united? Who are we partners with? Who are we partakers with? Where do we find enjoyment in life? Where do we look when we are searching for peace? Associations matter.

As a Christian, the spiritual application of this truth was unavoidable. There is a clear teaching throughout the New Testament that our associations are of utmost importance. This starts with the most basic association common to us all.

"...for all have sinned and fall short of the glory of God."
(Romans 3:23 ESV)

As created human beings we are all associated with the first man, Adam. This is a two-edged sword. Being Adam's descendants means both that we all bear the image of God and that we all share the guilt of the first sin against God. In Paul's letter to the Romans we learn that our association with Adam condemns us to death; we stand guilty before the absolute holiness of God. In this regard we truly are "guilty by association."

> *"For as by the one man's [Adam's] disobedience the many were made sinners, so by the one man's [Jesus'] obedience the many will be made righteous." (Romans 5:19 ESV)*

Fortunately, the story does not end with the guilt resulting from our association with Adam. Jesus Christ freely gives us the opportunity for innocence. Just as association with Adam brings death and slavery to sin, so association with Christ brings life and freedom from the power of sin. We really can be "innocent by association."

> *"... And be found in him [Christ], not having a righteousness of my own that comes from the law, but that which comes through faith in Christ, the righteousness from God that depends on faith." (Philippians 3:9 ESV)*

Innocence before God is not based upon performance (i.e., doing good or not doing bad). It is based on faith in Christ and connection with Christ. When we identify ourselves with Jesus, our wrongdoings no longer count against us, and we find forgiveness based upon His life, death, and resurrection. We get the reward that Christ has earned! On the other hand, if we continue to identify with the sin of Adam, being lovers of self rather than lovers of God, we are left to ourselves, separated from God and His salvation.

"I have been crucified with Christ. It is no longer I who live, but Christ who lives in me. And the life I now live in the flesh I live by faith in the Son of God, who loved me and gave himself for me." (Galatians 2:20 ESV)

This is the ultimate association—to be crucified with Christ, denying my short-sighted earthly desires, allowing Christ to live in me, and all this by faith in Jesus and His gift of inexpressible love. We are not just friends with Jesus. He is not a co-pilot or helper to guide us in life. He is not just an acquaintance or someone we rub spiritual shoulders with. The Bible says we can actually share in His death and resurrection and claim the victory that He won on our behalf. We are partakers with Christ!

"Therefore, if anyone is in Christ, he is a new creation. The old has passed away; behold, the new has come." (2 Corinthians 5:17 ESV)

Once we identify with Christ we are changed. The old association with sin and self passes away, and we are transformed into a new creation. Again, this is not a casual relationship. Being in Christ is the leaving of self for dead and clinging to the life that we can only find in Him.

Innocence by association with Jesus is an amazing gift. But it is a gift, and just like any other gift it has to be received to be realized. Just as we choose whom to associate with on a physical level (for example what company we keep), we also choose whether or not we will associate with Jesus. We are given the freedom to either embrace or reject the gift and the gift-giver.

So, then, I leave the old associations,

"...forgetting what lies behind and straining forward to what lies ahead, I press on toward the goal for the prize of

the upward call of God in Christ Jesus." (Philippians 3:13-14 ESV)

Reflection

❶ Is it natural to associate with Jesus?

❷ What kind of person was most drawn to Jesus during His life on earth?

- 24 -

THE GOOD CHRISTIAN

HAVE YOU EVER received a compliment that made you uncomfortable? This happened to me not too long ago when someone told me I was "good." Not as in "you're good at playing chess" (which I am not) but as in "you're a good person." It was actually meant to be a nice compliment, and I tried to receive it graciously. The reason I am uncomfortable about it is that it forced me to ask myself the serious question "Am I really 'good'? Unfortunately, I know myself much better than the person who paid me that compliment and do not come to the same conclusion. Let's take a moment to consider the following question: "Is there anyone—*anyone*—who is good (including Christians), and by what standard do we measure goodness?"

Jesus has a very high standard for what it means to be good. It is more than just an outward show; it is the actual state of the heart. In fact, the standard is so high that no person could ever achieve it. Jesus, who equated Himself with God, responded in this way to someone who called Him good:

> *"Why do you call me good? No one is good except God alone." (Luke 18:19 ESV)*

Teaching in a parable, Jesus told the story of the Pharisee and the Tax Collector at the Temple. The Pharisee was thanking God for how good he thought he was, and the Tax Collector cried out to God for mercy because he knew that he wasn't good. Jesus commended the man with the clear vision to see that he was broken, not the blinded man who thought he was good.

There is a perception that Christians are good. Or at least that they are *supposed to be* good. Or maybe that they think they are better than everyone else. The first step in becoming a Christian, however, is realizing that you are not good. The idea we can be good apart from God is a great deception that keeps many people from seeing their need for salvation. After all, if you are good on your own, what do you need God for? Only those who know they are broken will look for a remedy. The next step is understanding that all your good works as a Christian come not from you but from God. In fact, God says that He already has good works prepared for those who believe.

> *"For we are his workmanship, created in Christ Jesus for good works, which God prepared beforehand, that we should walk in them." (Ephesians 2:10 ESV)*

Every good work a Christian does is laid out beforehand by the careful planning of God Himself. Christians are simply fulfilling a role that was written by God long ago. Therefore, God gets all the glory.

So let's set the record straight: Christians are *not* good people. I am certainly not a good person. When I examine myself I find a broken man. Put bluntly, the Bible teaches that we are all bad people, as it says in Romans, "there is none righteous." Christians are simply those who recognize their emptiness and their need and run to a Savior who has offered them new life.

This is a primary example of worldview. How do you see yourself? Are you in need? Or are you good on our own? Depending on the glasses you are wearing, you may not realize that you are sick and in need of a physician. My impression is that virtually all people in our culture today sees themselves as "good people." We play a never-ending game of comparison between ourselves and those around us. Just like the Pharisee in Jesus' parable, we look at those in worse shape than ourselves and use that to prop up our faulty self-image. Again, as always, we have some choices: (1) we have it all together (at least we're better than our neighbor), or (2) it doesn't matter because life is pointless, or (3) we are broken and in need of fixing. Examine your own worldview carefully. Which choice best describes you?

Broken Man

I'm starting to realize I'm a broken man,
  And all I have to offer is an empty hand.
   My two legs are a shaky place to stand,
    So little control, life is not always what I planned.

In my mind I have the desire to drive,
  To direct my own path till I finally arrive.

Toward my own destination I constantly strive,
Thinking my will is what keeps me alive.

The closer I look at myself I find,
This life that I live is not really mine.
No control over health, wealth, or time,
Each day is a gift and I cannot rewind.

Inside my heart lies something not right,
This curse I cannot rid no matter how hard I fight.
At times my soul seems more dark and less light,
On my own there is no hope for salvation in sight.

There is a battle within and I can't seem to shake,
The influence of my unwanted roommate.
I need someone greater my soul to take,
To redeem and restore and completely remake.

O wretched man that I am,
Who will rescue me from this body of sin?
Then I hear the words of Jesus again,
Believe in me and your new life will have no end.

Jesus was broken so I could be whole,
He was crushed in order to save my soul.
And now while sin is still taking its toll,
I can look forward to the day with new life in full.

Now my life is free from the power of sin,
And one day God will take away its presence within.

O what a glorious and undeserved end,
    To spend eternity in the presence of Him.

Reflection

❶ Why are we humans so focused on performance? Do you compare yourself to others?

❷ Do you believe most people think of themselves as good? How do you tend to rate yourself on the goodness scale?

❸ What is the difference between God's standard and humans' standard when it comes to goodness?

COEXIST

IF YOU HAVE been out driving recently you have probably seen one of those creative COEXIST bumper stickers. COEXIST is spelled out very cleverly using symbols from world religions and philosophies. The message, of course, is one of unity. It is calling on all faiths to accept one another and live in harmony. It is a call for tolerance, each seeing the others' point of view as valid with no prejudice. We can all find our own path to God . . . or away from Him. There is no room for exclusion.

Every time I see this sticker it makes me uncomfortable. Here is a scenario to illustrate why: Have you been in a public building, maybe in a hallway or near an elevator, and seen a map directing people where to go in case of a fire? These maps are similar in most buildings. The first thing you see is an arrow with a large **YOU ARE HERE** to make sure you understand the starting point. Then there may be a red line indicating the safest route out of the building. It will steer you away from elevators and other dangers that may be present during an emergency. The purpose is to provide a safe exit out of the building.

Now imagine you are in such a building, on the tenth floor, when the fire alarm sounds. As you wait for an elevator, in panic you look around for a safe exit strategy. Then you spot the sign. Wonderful! You quickly scan the map, memorize the route, and start to head out. Just as you start to leave, however, you notice another sign just below the first, except this one has a different starting point and a different set of directions. As you glance across the hall you see yet a third sign with still another set of directions. Now you start to worry; the anxiety is mounting. The smell of smoke is filling the hallway. Some people come running past, and to your surprise they each glance quickly at different maps and then run off in three different directions. One jumps out the window, one gets on the elevator, and another disappears into an office suite down the hall. A fourth person hangs his head out a nearby doorway and shouts, "There is no danger! There never was a fire! False alarm!"

Yet the alarm is sounding, and the smoke is growing quite thick. Paralyzed, you stand in fear, not knowing what to do and waiting for rescue. Then you recall driving in to work that morning (it's funny what comes to mind during times of mortal danger) and seeing a COEXIST bumper sticker on a little car. "All paths lead to God" was the first thought that came to mind. If that's true of religions, too bad it doesn't apply to burning buildings. All paths shown on those maps cannot be safe. A woman just jumped out the window for crying out loud! There has to be *one* that is best and safe and *true*. But which one?

YOU ARE HERE. These three words are very important, not just on maps but in life. They allow us to get our bearings. A map is really quite useless if you don't know where you are to begin with. How can you get from here to there if you don't know where *here* is? All worldviews, whether theistic, atheistic, naturalistic, or even agnostic, start with these three small words. With these words we define our starting point in life. Each religion has a different idea of where to place the starting pin. The problem is that if we start wrong we will end wrong. Here are some examples:

- You are here – on a world formed purely by chance with no ultimate purpose.
- You are here – created by God with infinite value and purpose.
- You are here – as god of your own life determining your own destiny.
- You are here – to serve and follow Allah – or else.
- You are here – resulting from the deeds done in a previous life.
- You are here – where truth is relative and only a matter of opinion.
- You are here – the universe is divine essence and we are all god.
- You are here – there is an absolute truth to be discovered.
- You are here – there is no god.

It is clear these starting points are very different. Are they all accurate and reliable to guide us as we walk through this life? Some are diametrically opposed to one another. This means they cannot all be true.

Despite what our culture may tell us, truth does exist and can be found. Even without putting forth a case for any of the viewpoints listed above, any reasonable person can see that they simply cannot **all** be true. Some are exclusive of the others by definition. That is the nature of truth; it excludes everything that is not true. Truth, by definition, is intolerant. In other words, we cannot all be right!

What did Jesus say about truth?

> *"I am the way, and the truth, and the life. No one comes to the Father except through me." (John 14:6 ESV)*

And God, speaking to Isaiah, said:

> *"I am the Lord, and there is no other, besides me there is no God." (Isaiah 45:5 ESV)*

These are exclusive statements that are intolerant of other viewpoints. There is only one God and the only path that leads to Him is Jesus Christ.

There are two simple reasons I believe the Christian view of God to be true above all others:

1. We live in an obviously created universe that reveals that God does exist.
2. Jesus Christ rose from the dead after He was crucified. This is historically documented and the only scenario that fits the events surrounding the early Christian church. If He rose from the dead, then everything He said is true.

"Exclusive" and "intolerant" are not popular words. But when it comes to finding your way out of a burning building or obtaining eternal salvation for your soul it would be wise to seek the one true path, forsaking all others as folly, and encourage others to join you.

Now what about coexisting? Christians are called to love all people no matter what their belief system may be. Christians are also called to speak the truth in love, showing others the safe exit from the burning building. There is one truth found in Jesus Christ. Accepting many religions as valid and true has the same outcome as trying to follow contradicting escape routes – confusion and ultimately destruction.

When I use the term "intolerant" as a Christian I simply mean that I cannot accept all positions on all subjects as equally valid. That is, I believe in truth. The fact is, even though it might be offensive to some, truth by definition is intolerant. I harbor no malevolence toward those who hold an alternate view. I do not wish to force those who disagree with me into accepting my position. The Christian perspective is this: Truth is real and God has revealed Himself to us through creation, Scripture, and the life of Jesus. God loves you and wants to have a relationship with you. There is refreshment for your thirsty soul here. I would only seek to show you from where to draw the water.

Reflection

❶ Is it possible for all truth to be relative?

❷ Is it unloving to teach an absolute truth?

❸ Who has the final say in what is true and false?

– 26 –

COKE, KLEENEX, & CHRISTIANS

I MAGINE YOURSELF SITTING at a picnic table in a park on a beautiful, sunny afternoon. Maybe you are at a family reunion, or an Independence Day celebration, or just spending some time relaxing with friends. You have eaten more than your fair share of chips and hotdogs and are feeling a little parched. Then you spot one of your buddies heading for the drinks. "Hey," you say, "would you grab me a Coke out of the cooler?"

"Sure, what kind?" comes the reply. "Looks like we've got root beer, Sprite, Mt. Dew, even some diet stuff. So which one do you want?" This is a little confusing to you.

"I thought I could just have a Coke. Do you have any of that?"

"Yeah, sure, but what kind?"

"Is there more than one kind of Coke?" This is getting complicated. "I'll have a Coke, as in Coca-Cola."

"Oh, sorry it doesn't look like we have any of that, but we do have some generic cola. Will that work? It's all the same anyway."

Now fast-forward to the winter months. You are on your way to the office "holiday" party (nobody has Christmas parties anymore – too offensive). It's December and of course time for the annual head cold you always seem to catch. You stop at a convenience store to pick up some Kleenex so you won't be caught trying to stop a runny nose with your bare hands. "Where's the Kleenex?" you ask the clerk, in a stuffy head, nasally voice. He lowers his brow, obviously a little annoyed at all the germs you're bringing into his store, and says, "We don't carry Kleenex any more – too expensive, but we do have soft facial tissue paper, some of it even has lotion in it!" You force your best smile as you lay the box on the checkout counter. "You know, it's all the same anyway," says the clerk, already scrubbing his hands with sanitizer as you walk toward the door.

Band-Aids or adhesive bandages? Cheerios or Toasted O's? There are so many similar products that seem to be the same, but we all know they are not. There is the original, and then there is the generic or cheapened version that closely resembles the original. The marketplace becomes confusing for customers who now have to sort through so many similar products. The loss of brand name for a company can be devastating to advertising and sales. After all, if everyone calls any old sticky bandage a "Band-Aid" then the "Band-Aid" brand loses its identity. It becomes more difficult to distinguish itself from its competitors because the verbiage is all mixed and muddy.

What happens when the verbiage surrounding Christians is mixed and muddy? Have you ever told someone you are a Christian and then heard the reply "me, too!" Well, that's great in one sense because it's always encouraging to meet a brother or sister in Christ. But, on the other hand, what do you mean when you say "Christian"? What does the other person mean? Odds are just about anyone you bump into in the United States will be a "Christian." In an ABC news poll from the summer of 2013 (http://abcnews.go.com/US/story?id=90356), 83% of the Americans surveyed called themselves "Christian."

This raises some important questions: Just what is a Christian? Are all "Christians" the same? Is there an original Christianity that comes from God, and then others that, while using some of the same elements and language, are cheapened versions, made by something or someone other than God? Or is there perhaps, as in the examples cited above, really no difference between them and all Christians (and all religions for that matter) are basically just the same?

What is a true, genuine Christian? This is a sensitive question because it implies that some have a true faith and others have a misplaced or false faith. How can we identify someone who is truly following Christ? Why is the Christian landscape so confusing?

Jesus said, "If you abide in my word, you are truly my disciples, and you will know the truth, and the truth will set you free" (John 8:31-32 ESV). Later in John He said, "I am the way, and the truth, and the life. No one comes to the Father except through me" (John 14:6 ESV).

There is a true Gospel. Jesus made it clear that He is *the only way* we can be reconciled to God. In his letter to the Galatians, the Apostle Paul said this regarding a false gospel:

> *"I am astonished that you are so quickly deserting him who called you in the grace of Christ and are turning to a differ-*

ent gospel – not that there is another one, but there are some who trouble you and want to distort the gospel of Christ. But even if we or an angel from heaven should preach to you a gospel contrary to the one we preached to you, let him be accursed." (Galatians 1:6-9 ESV)

If there is a true Gospel and a false gospel, then it follows that there must also be genuine Christians (who believe a true Gospel) and what I will call generic or misled Christians (who are deceived by a false gospel). Paul was very adamant with the Galatians in the above quote because he saw the danger that false teaching would pose to the newly formed Church. Sorting out distorted teaching from sound teaching was a challenge in the early Church and remains so to the present day.

Why all this turmoil in the Church? One reason is because Christians and Christianity are under attack.

"Put on the whole armor of God, that you may be able to stand against the schemes of the devil." (Ephesians 6:11)

The Bible teaches that the devil (Satan) is an enemy who hates followers of Christ and is scheming against them. A scheme is a crafty or secret plan of action. So think for a moment, what would you do if you were Satan? How would you seek to undermine and destroy Christians? It is impossible simply to eliminate those who would follow Christ (because of God's protection), but perhaps there are some other strategies that would be effective for diminishing believers and their impact in the world. Let's consider five possible methods of disrupting the Christian Church: deception, division, confusion, distortion, and counterfeiting.

Deception: Satan is the father of lies starting with The Lie that "you can be like God," which was first conceived in his heart when he sought to steal glory from the Father and then later when he presented it to Adam and Eve in the Garden. "When he lies, he speaks out of his own character, for he is a liar and the father of lies" (John 8:44 ESV). Deception is always part of his scheming. The New Testament writers knew this all too well and warned frequently about false teachers.

Division: Faction and division lead to confusion over the identity of the true believer. Division has been ever-present in the Church dating back to the split between Paul and Apollos, and now there are too many divisions to count. In the closing of Romans, Paul says,

> *"I appeal to you, brothers, to watch out for those who cause divisions and create obstacles contrary to the doctrine that you have been taught; avoid them. For such persons do not serve our Lord Christ, but their own appetites, and by smooth talk and flattery they deceive the hearts of the naïve." (Romans 16:17-18 ESV)*

Many people look at the divisions in churches and are so repelled that they stop attending altogether.

Confusion: Now to be clear, not all divisions in the church are due to heresy (false teaching), but regardless of the cause, the result is the same – confusion. A seeker may ask, "What kind of Christian should I become? There are so many different types. Which church should I attend? Do all of them teach the truth or just some?" From the outside looking in, the seeker has a strong basis for looking at the "Christian" Church and shaking his or her head in bewilderment and walking the other way. If you are one for scheming, this is a great one!

Distortion: As mentioned above, some false teachers distort the Gospel of Christ. In some ways this is more destructive than denying the core Gospel message altogether. Distortion takes things out of focus. It is a twisting of the truth. Adherents to a distorted Gospel message will be led to believe they have found the truth. Therefore, they will stop looking for truth. They have done well to abandon the sinking ship that this life represents but have been coaxed onto a lifeboat that has a fatal leak and will doom them in the end. This has to be one of the enemy's favorite tools – leading souls into a false security while taking them farther and farther away from God.

Counterfeit: What about those who say they are Christians but exhibit no evidence of any change occurring in their lives? What about the "hypocrites" whom Jesus so strongly condemned? Without being overly judgmental, it seems reasonable to say that not all who claim the name Christ are true Christians. In fact, Jesus warned that there would be imposters to sort out at the final judgment.

> *"Not everyone who says to me, 'Lord, Lord,' will enter the kingdom of heaven, but the one who does the will of my Father who is in heaven. On that day many will say to me, 'Lord, Lord, did we not prophesy in your name, and cast out demons in your name, and do many mighty works in your name?' And then will I declare to them, 'I never knew you; depart from me, you workers of lawlessness.'"*
> *(Matthew 7:21-23 ESV)*

What better plan than to overrun the true believers with counterfeits who cause the name of Jesus Christ damage and poor repute. There is a bumper sticker that goes something like this: "I love Christ, but I can't stand Christians."

Christians are not done growing. It is worth mentioning here that even those who abide in Christ and follow Him closely will fail and fail often. Every Christian is still at war with the flesh and that frequently causes stumbling. It is important to remember to keep our eyes turned vertically toward God rather than horizontally toward each other. God is the only One who will never disappoint.

There is a genuine Christianity. At times, it seems this world is saturated with generics. As Jesus said, true believers will be known by the fruit in their lives.

My prayer is that I may be found faithful not only in my belief but in my actions, and that I would "walk in a manner worthy of the Lord" so that my life would reflect His light and His glory.

Reflection

❶ Are you ever discouraged by the numerous kinds of "Christians" and Christian churches? Do you think all these "varieties" of Christians are a positive or a negative thing?

❷ If you were Satan, what would you do to disrupt the Church?

❸ Why are Christians so often accused of hypocrisy?

– 27 –

WHOSE LOVE ARE WE SHARING?

OUR FAMILY IS in the process of adopting two children from Haiti. I have been challenged to consider carefully my motives in seeking to bring these little ones into our lives. Is it because my heart is filled with love? Well, the answer to that question is yes and no. My heart is filled with love, but only that which has overflowed from the heart of my heavenly Father. God loves these little children, and He has moved us to share His love through adoption.

Father God,
  One in Trinity.
    With ever spreading goodness,
      Adopted a soul like me.

In constant fellowship,
  You are able to love.

The eternal relationship,
For me too high above.

With spoken word created all,
Love spreading to all things.
And even after Adam's fall,
Mercy through the Son You bring.

Unable in my flesh,
To seek and do Your will.
With Your Spirit refresh,
My heart and soul to fill.

But my heart can be hard,
Sometimes it seems like stone.
Give me loving regard,
For those who have no home.

The source of love now overflows,
Filling up Your own.
Enabling hearts opposed to You,
To give the fatherless a home.

Not turning away Your gaze,
From little ones in need.
The orphans lonely days,
Pass not Your sight unseen.

In fragile vessels like myself,
Spreading goodness is Your way.
To help me love someone else,
In my family now to stay.

"God's goodness is a communicative, spreading goodness. . . . If God had not a communicative, spreading goodness, he would never have created the world. The Father, Son and Holy Ghost were happy in themselves and enjoyed one another before the world was. But that God delights to communicate and spread his goodness, there had never been a creation nor a redemption. God useth his creatures not for defect of power, that he can do nothing without them, but for the spreading of his goodness. . . ."

—Richard Sibbes 1577-1635 (Italics added)

Reflection

❶ Where do goodness and love originate?

❷ Who is getting the glory when we share the love God has placed in us?

❸ What happens when we rely on ourselves as the source of love?

JUST OUT OF REACH

TIGER WOODS AND I have one thing in common: We are both unhappy with our golf scores. Now, to be clear, Tiger is in the conversation regarding who is the best professional golfer of all time, and I am just a below-average golfer who doesn't even play regularly. Tiger's ultimate goal seems to be besting Jack Nicklaus for the most major tournament wins of all time, while my goal is to break a score of 100 on occasion. We both have things to be proud of. I occasionally hit a good shot or make a par, and he has won many professional tournaments and made millions of dollars during his career.

We both have accomplishments, mine rather small, and his very impressive, but we are still unsatisfied. He still shouts in disgust when he hits an errant shot and seems disappointed if he does not win each tour event he plays. I walk off the course wondering why I haven't improved at all since the last time I played. I used to believe that I would enjoy golfing more if I was just a little bit better. After watching the professionals, however, I realized that "a little bit better" is always just "a little out of reach."

Isn't the same thing true in our lives? We have a vision for the way life should be. We want to be happy. We want satisfaction. We set goals. But somehow the achievement of those goals is not quite what we expected.

No matter what the level, human accomplishment leaves us unsatisfied and wishing for more. It doesn't matter if we step over molehills or scale mountains, there is always something elusive in our achievements. Satisfaction and contentment are hard to find. True happiness seems to be the carrot that dangles just a few inches out of reach no matter how fast or how far we run.

This leaves us in a very precarious situation in which we can never quite achieve the happiness we so desire. Each peak we conquer may provide a temporary sense of satisfaction, but soon we find ourselves looking for more. Could this be why the rich and famous among us, our celebrities, are so prone to substance abuse, depression, relational strife, and suicide or accidental death? Shouldn't these people be happy given their material wealth and status in life? They have fame, fortune, privilege—the very best this world has to offer—and yet find it a very disturbing disappointment. No one in the Bible—perhaps no one in history—sought happiness and pleasure with more vigor than King Solomon. And his conclusion was an indictment of the pursuit as "vanity," as futile as chasing after the wind.

Consider this quote from Green Bay Packers quarterback Aaron Rodgers commenting on his feelings after winning the Super Bowl following the 2010 NFL season:

"I remember sitting on the bus after we won in [Arlington, Texas], probably two hours after the game, thinking to myself, 'I'm on top of the world. We just accomplished the most amazing goal in football.' But I'm sitting there with a semi-empty feeling because I accomplished everything I wanted to do since I was a kid, and I kind of had a moment. 'I said to myself, "Is this it? Is there more to life than this?"'" (www.humanosphere.org/basics/2014/01/nfl-superstar-campaigns-dr-congo/)

While my accomplishments in life are small compared to some, I have accomplished enough to know that my personal achievements will never make me happy. My financial standing is meager compared to some, but I have earned enough money to figure out that I will always want "just a little more." I have looked at those "ahead of" or "above" me in life and concluded that the view from up there is not all it's cracked up to be.

Some may say, "But that's just human nature, we all strive to get more out of life!" And I would say, "Exactly!" The nature of humans is to seek that which satisfies. That is the way God made us. The problem is that satisfaction can *never* be found outside of a relationship with Jesus Christ. Our hearts were made for contented satisfaction. The challenge is to figure out what it is that really fills us up. As C. S. Lewis put it:

"If I find in myself desires which nothing in this world can satisfy, the only logical explanation is that I was made for another world."

My prayer is that I would live a life of contentment, no matter what my level of accomplishment is according to the world's standards and be looking forward to the day when all things will be made new and I will spend eternity in the presence of my Savior completely and fully satisfied in Him.

> *".....not that I am speaking of being in need, for I have learned in whatever situation I am to be content. I know how to be brought low, and I know how to abound. In any and every circumstance, I have learned the secret of facing plenty and hunger, abundance and need. I can do all things through him who strengthens me." (Philippians 4:11-13 ESV)*

Reflection

❶ Why is happiness in this life so elusive?

❷ Is it possible to be truly happy apart from God? What about the "happy and content atheist"? Is it a myth?

❸ Why is contentment seen as a negative in our culture today?

– 29 –

WHICH WAY IS UP?

THE KINGDOM OF Heaven is an upside-down place where servants are kings, the mourning are happy, the poor are rich, and the guilty receive grace.

It is a place where the first become last and the last become first, the humble heart is lifted up and the proud heart is brought low, the strong are made weak and the weak are made strong, the wise counted as foolish and the foolish counted as wise.

The Kingdom of Heaven goes against intuition, against the predictable, against human nature, and against our first instinct. Not only the citizens embody this paradox, but even the King humbled Himself beyond imagination, coming as a baby into the world He created, seeking the lost, serving the outcasts, washing the feet of His disciples, and dying a criminal's death He did not deserve.

If this is God's way then which direction is up? Does the creation see life more clearly than the Creator? The Kingdom of

Heaven is not an upside-down place, but rather a true representation of what God has intended. This leaves our world the backward place, depravity twisting the mind and blinding the eyes, making us unable to see the ultimate reality.

Happy Ones

It is good to be poor in spirit,
  Before God bowing low.
    Blessed are those who hear it,
      Jesus Christ told me so.

The happy are filled with mourning,
  Upon seeing their great need.
    Yet blessings found each morning,
      There is forgiveness indeed.

The gentle are called meek,
  Not asserting their own will.
    The Kingdom first to seek,
      An inherited earth to fill.

God is the source of righteousness,
  Satisfying the hungry soul.
    Quenching the thirst for uprightness,
      Making a person whole.

Those who mercy freely give,
  Imitating the Father's love.
    Reserving judgment as they live,
      Are shown great mercy from above.

When the heart is clean within,
  The external show is put away.

Only then can they see Him,
Shining like the light of day.

Peacemakers are God's sons,
Seeking on earth and heaven his will.
Truly they are blessed ones,
Hearing his voice, "Peace be still."

Happy are those by others reviled,
For speaking the Savior's name.
A great reward in being God's child,
In eternity theirs to claim.

Matthew 5:1-12

Reflection

❶ When God's view of happiness differs from our own, who should we believe?

❷ Read the Sermon on the Mount found in Matthew chapters 5-7. Why was this teaching so revolutionary?

30

FADING

*"Apart from God, everything is fading, but through Jesus
all who believe, He is saving."*

FADING

Remembering who won the Super Bowl,
*   Fresh new paint that now seems dull,*
*   Head of hair that once was full,*
*   Patience through life's daily pull.*

FADING

The shine of a once-new car,
*   Memories from travels afar,*
*   Solace found at the bar,*
*   The glory of being a star.*

FADING

A wedding's joyful beginning,
 A funeral's sober ending,
  The satisfaction of winning,
   Temporary pleasure of sinning.

FADING

The hope that money brings,
 A life that's focused on things,
  The song that pleasure sings,
   The beauty of many rings.

FADING

Man knows not his time,
 His span of days he cannot find,
  While living in this world so blind,
   Focused on the muddy grime.

FADING

Think deeper and lift up your eyes,
 What comes next after everyone dies,
  Stop seeking an earthly prize,
   The wind you are chasing is nothing but lies.

FADING

But for God all is in vain,
 If Christ never came,
  It is all one big game,
   No winners, all losers, we all end the same.

SAVING

Do not stick your head in the sand,
    Nor put your face in your hands,
        Wake up so you might understand,
            God's merciful salvation plan.

SAVING

God offers forgiveness,
    A light shining in darkness,
        He leads lives into fullness,
            By the grace of His goodness.

SAVING

He loves and forgives us,
    Renews and restores us,
        His blood was spilt for us,
            So join in the chorus.

SAVING

There is joy in this life,
    It was given at great price,
        Look forward to the end of strife,
            The gift of eternal life.

"O, LORD, make me know my end and what is the measure of my days; let me know how fleeting I am . . . man heaps up wealth and does not know who will gather!" (Psalm 39:5-6)

Reflection

❶ What are you holding onto that will fade?

❷ Is there any security to be found in life?

❸ Can you remember a once-new prized possession that is now garbage?

31

RESOLVED TO THINK ABOUT DEATH

I VISITED A CEMETERY recently for a graveside memorial. After celebrating the life of our loved one, I took some time to walk the cemetery grounds, stopping to read many of the names and captions on the headstones. These were real people with real lives, some very short and others quite long. Each one ran a race; for some it was a sprint, for others a marathon. The decisions each person made while living now echo through eternity. At this moment, some are enjoying the presence of God and others are separated from Him forever. During my walk, I was reminded to think about death. Why? Because thinking about death changes the way I will live my life. I want to finish strong whether that is tomorrow or 50 years from now. I agree with the great colonial preacher Jonathan Edwards who said that pondering the end of life helps us to better use the time we are given in faithful service to God. Edwards wrote that he was "Resolved, to

think much on all occasions of my own dying, and of the
common circumstances which attend death."

I am resolved to think about death.
 None of us know the days we have left.
  The future is uncertain, just like the next breath.
   It is in God's hands and this gives me rest.

This life is a course that each one must run.
 Endure day by day, that the prize may be won.
  Follow Jesus, God's only begotten Son.
   He upholds and strengthens each faltering one.

Running with purpose to finish the race,
 Looking forward, but still keeping the pace.
  Breaking the tape, and finally seeing His face.
   Entering His gates, completely by grace.

Death's thought may seem a morbid meditation,
 But it leads to a life lived with new dedication.
  Serving with joy the God of creation,
   Thankful each day for the gift of salvation.

*"Do you not know that in a race all the runners run, but
only one receives the prize? So run that you may obtain it."
(1 Corinthians 9:24 ESV)*

Reflection

❶ Why are we so hesitant to talk about death? Why do we humans tend to be in "death denial"?

❷ Because of modern advancements in medicine people in developed countries such as the United States are seldom exposed to death compared to previous generations. How does this change our perspective on life?

32

REFLECTING ON REFLECTION

I DISCOVERED REFLECTION AS a child. I remember seeing an unexpected point of light dancing across the wall in the middle of the day. Being familiar with flashlights, my natural assumption was that someone was shining a light on the wall. But a quick glance around the room confirmed that I was alone. The light seemed to move erratically, not following any pattern I could make out. The longer I watched, the more I began to have this eerie feeling that somehow I was connected to this phenomenon. To my surprise, I shifted in my chair, and the light disappeared. Moving back to my original spot, I was pleased, and a little taken back, that the little spot reappeared as strong and bright as ever.

It was not until I moved my arm slowly, and watched in amazement as the light on the wall followed, that I realized the light was coming from me. Looking down I saw my favorite hand-me-down wristwatch with a smooth plastic face. The light was coming from my watch! I quickly learned how to direct the light wherever I wished. At that point, I had a brilliant idea. I did what all kids do when they have a new glow-in-the-dark toy or flashlight—run to the bathroom where there are no windows, turn off the lights, and try it out. To my great disappointment there was no light shining in the dark bathroom. It stayed black, dark, and boring. It was only then that I discovered reflection. I learned that the light was not coming from my watch but rather from the sun. My watch was just the reflector. There was absolutely no light present in my watch by itself; it only reflected the shining brightness of the sun.

As hard as it is to accept, the Bible teaches that we human beings are just like my watch. There is no light in us, only darkness. It is hard to accept this because we would like to believe that deep down we are capable, independent, in charge, and *good*. Jeremiah put it well when he wrote "The heart is deceitful above all things, and desperately sick; who can understand it?" (Jeremiah 17:9 ESV). At first glance this statement seems extreme and unnecessary . . . until we consider Jesus' teaching in the Sermon on the Mount (Matthew chapters 5-7). If after reading Jesus' words your heart is not convicted of adultery, murder, lying, and selfishness (just to name a few), then you are not being honest.

In Romans, Paul quoted Isaiah's writing, "None is righteous, no, not one…" (Romans 3:10 ESV). He is establishing the fact that all people, whether Jew or Gentile, are in need of a savior because we all fall short of God's glory. Later in Romans Paul personalizes this theme when he writes:

> *"For I know that nothing good dwells in me, that is, in my flesh. For I have the desire to do what is right, but not the ability to carry it out." (Romans 7:18 ESV)*

The wisdom in Proverbs teaches:

"As in water face reflects face, so the heart of man reflects the man." (Proverbs 27:19 ESV)

We have taken a brief biblical survey of the heart in the above passages, and it certainly does not reflect well on man. It would seem there is something profoundly and foundationally wrong with us when we are left on our own.

"For God, who said, 'Let light shine out of darkness,' has shone in our hearts to give the light of the knowledge of the glory of God in the face of Jesus Christ." (2 Corinthians 4:6 ESV)

The God who spoke light into the absolute darkness, when the earth was without form and void (Genesis 1:2), now shines the light of His love into the darkness of the human heart. "…For at one time you were darkness, but now you are light in the Lord. Walk as children of light…" (Ephesians 5:8 ESV). It is interesting to note here that Paul does not say at one time you *were in darkness*, but at one time you *were darkness*. I wasn't just previously living in darkness but rather was the darkness itself, with nothing in me to commend myself to God. I would echo Paul here in crying out, "Wretched man that I am! Who will deliver me from this body of death?" (Romans 7:24 ESV).

We were not created to be the source of light. The Bible says we cannot be good by ourselves. We were created to be reflectors. Jesus did call his followers to be lights in this world (Matthew 5:14), but we can only shine if He has given us the light of His life. "I am the light of the world. Whoever follows me will not walk in darkness, but will have the light of life" (John 8:12 ESV). Just as the face of my watch had to turn toward the light in order to shine so must we turn our faces toward Jesus Christ and allow His love to shine in us and through us.

"God shows his love for us in that while we were still sinners, Christ died for us" (Romans 5:8 ESV). God is the source, overflowing with love, and ready to reveal Himself to those He has chosen. We are ultimately responders. "We love because he first loved us" (1 John 4:19 ESV). We do not first love God. Our first inclination is to love ourselves, not others, and certainly not God. We do not choose God. He chooses us! "…If God so loved us, we also ought to love one another" (1 John 4:11 ESV).

So why does any of this matter? It matters because it defines our relationship with God. In fact, it even defines the character of God Himself! Who exactly is doing the seeking? Is it man seeking God or God seeking man? Where does the potential for good reside? Is it in fallen human beings or does it always begin with God? Why does God love me? Is it because I have reached a level of achievement or is it because of God's overflowing love in spite of my failures? In the end, what matters to God is relationship. He is relational. He is the Good Shepherd seeking the lost sheep. He is the faithful husband loving the adulterous wife. He is willing to give the life of His Son to restore the relationship that was lost in the Garden so long ago. He is the light that would penetrate the darkness found inside each one of us—not just to expose our sin for what it is but to bring us into a loving relationship with Himself.

I am driven to my knees in humble adoration of a God who would seek me out, even as I lay dead in sin and darkness and in open opposition to His will, and not only that, but that He would offer up Himself to suffer the penalty that my sin required. And after breathing life into my spirit, He shines His light into my life so that I have the opportunity to share that light with others. My prayer is that God will continue to reveal Himself to me as I spend time in His Word, so that I might reflect the light of His love more clearly.

Reflection

❶ Can we do anything good apart from God?

❷ Do you think God evaluates us based on our "goodness"?

❸ Is it surprising that the Bible teaches that without God there is only darkness in us?

- 33 -

PURSUED

Pursued

Inherited sin's wages on the day of my birth,
    Though alive, I was dead from my first days on earth.
        Yet despite this You loved me and found in me
            worth,
                Before time you saw me and planned a rebirth.

Content in my lost state, I searched not for you.
    Satisfied in myself, I had no long-term view.
        Looking at generations, seeing all the way through,
            You found me and chose me in love to pursue.

Nothing I earned or worked to receive,
    It is all about Christ and what He did for me.
        Before God, not my life, but Jesus He sees.
            My only response is, "Lord, how can this be?"

Pursued and adopted as God's special one,
Even though it cost Him the life of the Son.
Not complete, but a heavenward journey begun;
Looking forward to that day, when at last He
has come.

Reflection

❶ The Bible says that God pursues us even though we rejected Him. What does that tell you about God?

❷ If this is true, how can it be that some still refuse to accept God's great gift?

CONCLUSION

THE SKEPTIC AND the believer alike should carefully consider the following question: *What if it's true?* Take some time to think about this. What if God created us, loves us, and is offering us a restored relationship with Him through Jesus Christ? What if this life that we experience is just the beginning of something much bigger? Could it be that death is not the end? Will the decisions we make today impact our eternal destiny?

For the skeptic, missing out on the reality of God means that you miss out on a relationship with God. It means you will be separated from God forever as the consequence of your own decisions. It seems obvious that any skeptic should spend some time carefully evaluating his or her position, but isn't the same thing true for the believer?

For those who believe: Is your belief intellectual, or do you believe with all your heart, soul, mind, and strength? Do you find yourself just going through the motions, or is the reality of Jesus actually changing your life? How would your outlook change if you fully grasped the love of a God who would humble Himself beyond measure, take on the punishment you deserved, die on the cross in your place, pay the debt you owed, free you from sin and separation, and prepare for you an inheritance in Heaven (and all this while you were hostile toward Him)?

Speaking personally, I do believe, but not always in sufficient measure. Christians are not perfect in faith or in deed. I pray the magnitude of what God has done will be more real to me each day. At times I echo Mark 9:24 in crying out, "I believe, help my unbelief!"

How does this affect worldview?

Is God the Creator who is loving and relational, seeking to save and redeem those who are lost? Or is He distant, angry, inept, cruel, or imaginary? After reading this book, I hope you have examined your own worldview. My prayer is that you have a different or renewed perspective of who God is, as well as a different or renewed perspective of who you are. I hope that you have taken some time to meditate on God and that you have been motivated to look deeper into His Word.

"What comes into our minds when we think about God is the most important thing about us." This is our worldview. It is the way we interpret life. Actually, *world*view would be better stated as *God*view, because that is what it truly represents. The way we view God changes everything. In life, these are **The Glasses We Wear.**

18207526R00094

Made in the USA
San Bernardino, CA
04 January 2015